Forgotten Conservatives
in American History

Forgotten Conservatives *in* American History

Brion McClanahan and Clyde N. Wilson

PELICAN PUBLISHING COMPANY
Gretna 2012

Copyright © 2012
By Brion McClanahan and Clyde N. Wilson
All rights reserved

The word "Pelican" and the depiction of a pelican are trademarks of Pelican Publishing Company, Inc., and are registered in the U.S. Patent and Trademark Office.

Library of Congress Cataloging-in-Publication Data

McClanahan, Brion T.
  Forgotten conservatives in American history / by Brion McClanahan and Clyde N. Wilson.
    p. cm.
  Includes index.
  ISBN 978-1-4556-1579-7 (hardcover : alk. paper) – ISBN 978-1-4556-1580-3 (e-book) 1. Conservatives–United States–Biography. 2. Conservatism–United States–History–Biography. I. Wilson, Clyde Norman. II. Title.
  JC573.2.U6M365 2012
  320.52092'273–dc23
                      2012001778

Printed in the United States of America
Published by Pelican Publishing Company, Inc.
1000 Burmaster Street, Gretna, Louisiana 70053

To those who fight for the Principles of '76 and '98, present and future:

*In the words of the immortal Stonewall,
"Forward, gentlemen, and show them the bayonet."*

Table of Contents

Acknowledgements	9
Introduction	11
James Jackson: Forgotten Founding Father	17
John Taylor of Caroline: Thomas Jefferson at Home	25
The Bayards of Delaware: America's Conservative Family	35
James Fenimore Cooper: The Aristocrat as Democrat	49
Condy Raguet: Apostle of Free Trade and Free Banking	61
True American Whiggery: John Tyler and Abel P. Upshur	73
"A Senator of Rome When Rome Survived:" The Unknown Calhoun	85
Grover Cleveland: The Last Jeffersonian President	95
William Graham Sumner and "The Forgotten Man"	105
E. L. Godkin and the Ideal American	117
War and Money: The Lindberghs of Minnesota	129
H. L. Mencken as Conservative	141
James Gould Cozzens: Conscience, Duty, and Love	147
Citizen Faulkner: "What We Did, In Those Old Days"	151
Sam Ervin: The Last Constitutionalist	157
M. E. Bradford and the American Founding	169
A Mass for the Resurrection: Who Owns America?	179
Bibliography	189
Index	193

Acknowledgments

In 1997, I traveled to the University of South Carolina to tour the campus and meet Dr. Clyde Wilson. I was soon to graduate with a BA in History from Salisbury University, and I had great professors and mentors there, most importantly Dr. Bart Talbert, but I did not yet realize that I knew very little history. It was not their fault. I was twenty-one and naïve. After meeting Dr. Wilson for a few minutes, two of his students, Carey Roberts and John Devanny, took me to a room and interrogated me, asking questions ranging from why I wanted to go to graduate school, to why I wanted to work with Dr. Wilson, to what I thought of various people in American history. I guess I passed, because the next fall, Dr. Wilson took me on as one of his students, and ultimately his last doctoral student.

I finally learned a little history and in the process made a good friend. I would not be where I am today without Dr. Wilson's tutelage. The same can be said for almost two dozen other fine historians, and by default anyone who has read his works or those that have been produced by his students, the present volume included. I say this for all of his students and those who have been influenced or mentored by his thoughtful guidance, thank you. I am honored to be the first, and hopefully not the last, of his students to write a work of history with him.

I would also like to thank the library staff at Chattahoochee Valley Community College, notably Xueying Chen and Corey Williams, and the library staff at Columbus State University for their help in this project.

Brion McClanahan
24 January 2012, Phenix City, Alabama

Introduction

Several times in his dense treatises, John Taylor of Caroline, the systematic philosopher of Jeffersonian democracy, warned that political terms are treacherous and their exact meaning must be examined with care. Because, words are themselves weapons in the eternal campaign of designing men to achieve power and exploit their fellows. Let them control the terms of the debate and you have already conceded the battle.

Not only are political terms subject to deceptive use, but their connotations are inevitably relative and change with time and circumstances. So it is with "liberal" and "conservative." During the second half of the twentieth century those terms fairly clearly described a division in the American polity. One had a pretty good idea of the difference between a "liberal" and a "conservative" and could predict which way either might jump. That is no longer the case.

Beginning with the upheavals of the Sixties, for obvious reasons the number of people who called themselves "liberals" began to decline and "conservative" self-identification began to rise from a long spell in the doldrums. There was a great deal of discussion of exactly what "conservatism" is. There were traditionalists, libertarians, anti-communists, and others who agreed on a need to challenge the dominant liberal regime. The argument over what constituted an American conservative was never concluded. It was pre-empted by the rise to power of "neo-conservatives" under the wings of Ronald Reagan.

Soon the "neoconservatives" became the accepted, respectable Right in American discourse and the erstwhile conservatives became an irrelevant and possibly dangerous fringe, disdained equally by all decent people, whether "liberal" or "conservative." The new conservatives, however, were a rather peculiar band to carry that name. They were Trotskyites who had replaced their hereditary agenda of global socialist revolution with one of a global revolution of "democratic capitalism." Unashamedly embracing Machiavellian tactics against opponents and against the American people, they gloried in "big government" and fervently planned to project American armed force around the world, the national debt be damned. None of this could be considered a "conservative" agenda or way of proceeding.

This was hardly what the millions of "conservatives" who voted for Reagan, the self-declared enemy of big government, had bargained for. However, it was probably inevitable given the political ineptitude and naïve decency of conservative leadership; given that Republicans had always had a weakness for moralistic crusading; and given that "neo-conservatism" did not much bother the state capitalist elite, who really control the Republican party. It could even be boasted that now the Republicans had the guidance of bona fide "intellectuals" whom they had so long lacked (though the claim of William Bennett and other neo-conservative luminaries to the status of "intellectual" might be questioned).

We have chosen to be guided by Russell Kirk's classic *The Conservative Mind* in identifying who is a conservative. According to Kirk's once-honored teaching, a conservative is one who values "prescription," that is, who defers more to established custom and wisdom than to rational speculation, who insists that inevitable change should be cautious and reconcilable with the wisdom of the ages. A conservative avoids being a "provincial in time," recognizing a responsibility to the past and the future; he would not willingly burden future generations with debt by spending up everything for present notions and pleasures. An American conservative will certainly honor the true "Constitution for the United States" as it was before greed, ambition, ignorance, and deceit distorted it beyond all recognition. An American conservative naturally remembers the warnings of the most revered forefathers about "entangling alliances" with foreigners.

A conservative tends to value voluntary community, a larger sphere for private society, and a smaller sphere for government, especially the federal government. Fundamentally, a conservative is one who accepts that the world was endowed by its Creator with an enduring moral order (as described by C. S. Lewis in *The Abolition of Man*). In his love of Creation a conservative delights in the proliferating variety of life among free people, the direct opposite of "multiculturalism," which is an enforced monolithic non-culture. A conservative knows as well that man is forever imperfect, that evil comes in many comely guises, and that not all "progress" is progress.

Thus the duty of a conservative in politics, society, and culture is to exercise what Kirk called "the moral imagination," to keep in touch and in tune with the moral order to which all questions must ultimately be referred and to which the giants of the past, upon whose shoulders we stand, have pointed the way.

In understanding conservatism in American history one must avoid a common confusion. In America, Kirk pointed out, an acquisitive impulse has often been mistaken for a conservative disposition. Thus there is a frequent erroneous identification of conservatism with capitalist interests. Conservatives generally believe in the necessity of private property for civilization and accept the utility of free markets for general prosperity. That does not necessarily make them support corporate welfare or international conglomerates, which can be as destructive of social order as socialism and have a dubious relation to true private property and free enterprise.

By this measure, the American regime today cannot be considered to be to any significant degree "conservative." The United States in the early twenty-first century, in fact, has no politics at all in the strict sense. Presidential elections do not address real issues but revolve around personalities. Congressmen are elected according to their adroitness in delivering the pork and are careful to leave all important and potentially divisive decisions to the president and the U.S. Supreme Court.

Both parties are in essential agreement on a settled, semi-imperial order and they can hardly be told apart. Both are eager to please Wall Street and happy to let the masters of media set the terms of national discourse. Both are content with a government that brings more and more of our life under federal control. Neither seems to think that a military presence in more than one hundred countries or a catastrophic national debt are anything to worry about. Both are committed to the ongoing demographic and cultural transformation of the American population by mass immigration. Both are in the process of legitimizing changes in age-old morality of sexual roles and practices, although at a different pace.

It might be timely then to pay some attention to some of the numerous admirable people who have exemplified and preached forgotten conservative ideas. The men we have chosen do not agree completely among themselves. That is no problem, because conservatism as defined by Russell Kirk is not an ideology or a fixed program but a "disposition." All of our subjects exemplify some lost aspect of American thought. Often they will be seen to be prophets as well as sages.

Forgotten Conservatives
in **American History**

James Jackson:
Forgotten Founding Father

James Jackson did not sign the Declaration of Independence or the Constitution. But his heroism in the War of Independence and his exemplary integrity and republican statesmanship in the first days of the U.S. government entitle him to rank with the great men of the founding generation.

Jackson is a fine example of what that generation and several subsequent generations of Americans regarded as republican virtue. Virtue in this connection did not refer to private morals. It referred to the type of character deemed necessary to preserve liberty, a thing of great value to the community and the individual. It had a masculine Roman cast, which is why we have classical capitol buildings and statues of George Washington in a toga.

Republican virtue implied a tough, independent citizen ready to defend his society against foreign threats. Equally important, it was characterized by the wisdom to discern and the courage to oppose threats to liberty from inside society. History has furnished many examples of the undermining of free governments by plausible, designing men ambitious for power and profit. This is why Thomas Jefferson said that eternal vigilance is the price of liberty and that the tree of liberty needs to be watered from time to time with the blood of tyrants and patriots. A virtuous republican had the makings of such a patriot.

A patriot did not seek public fame and fortune. His task was alertness to preserve the principles of free government against all comers. He did not seek power, but if called to public office he took it as a duty to his society, not as an opportunity for self-advancement. His ambition was for his country, not himself. The example here was the Roman hero Cincinnatus, who was called from his farm to lead an army and having won the victory went home and resumed his plowing. Though not always put purely into practice, this ideal was a powerful influence in early American politics. As Forrest

McDonald, the leading historian of the early Union, has pointed out, in New England and the regions it influenced, republican virtue had a slightly more Puritan and less classical aura and included an emphasis on profitable economic activity and community supervision of private morals. Different conceptions of republican virtue would prove to be a rub when James Jackson joined the very first session of the United States Congress.

James Jackson was born in 1757 in Devonshire, England. At the age of fifteen he sailed the Atlantic unaccompanied and landed in 1772 at Savannah, Georgia, where some family friends were living. Despite his youth and his recent arrival from the mother country, Jackson enthusiastically joined the cause of American independence. Throughout the war he was active in military service. After the British capture of Savannah, Jackson escaped, reportedly swam the Savannah River, and arrived barefoot and in tatters to join the South Carolina patriot forces as a private, serving seventeen months with Thomas Sumter's partisans. He took part in most of the fighting in the Southern colonies and in expeditions into Florida and to the Indian frontier. He was wounded at least once and repeatedly cited for gallantry and enterprise. Jackson ended the war as a twenty-four-year-old lieutenant colonel in command of his own battalion and was selected to receive the official surrender of Savannah from the departing British on July 11, 1782.

After the war Jackson established himself as a successful lawyer and planter. Georgia was the smallest of the states in population and settled territory (though already filling fast with new settlers), and it had an exposed frontier. It quickly ratified the proposed Constitution for the United States without the reservations that concerned many and kept North Carolina out of the Union for several more years. In 1788 the Georgia legislature elected Jackson governor. He declined on grounds that he was too inexperienced for the august position. The next year he was elected as one of Georgia's two representatives to the First Congress. Shipwrecked on his way to New York, he arrived too late for the inaugural day but was soon an outspoken member of the House.

Jackson found the House discussing the proper way to address the president, with proposals like "His Excellency," "His Grace," and "His Serene Highness" being offered by those who wanted to endow the new government with dignity and awe. Jackson's republican blood boiled over. He ridiculed such talk and lamented that some of it was coming from Boston, "a town which, fifteen years ago, would have acknowledged no Lord but the Lord of hosts." He won his point, though some opponents hinted that the representative from Georgia was too loud and crude. "I have accustomed myself to a blunt integrity of speech," Jackson told the House, "which I hope the goodness of my intentions will excuse." The more serious criticisms of the representative from Georgia were uttered in private. It was known that Jackson had more than once taken his stand on the Savannah dueling ground and had always walked away.

When the First Congress convened, there were no party lines and there was a great deal of policy and practice for which precedents needed to be established. In this situation, Treasury Secretary Alexander Hamilton and his friends took the initiative with what would after awhile be revealed as a determined agenda for the future of the Union. The first move came in Hamilton's proposal to pay off the Continental debt of the Revolution. Everyone agreed that the debt had to be retired, but the devil was in the details. Hamilton's plan was to pay the holders of the debt in interest-bearing government bonds, thus to create a permanent public debt, which would in turn require tax revenue.

There was an even-more-serious kicker. The debt was to be funded at face value. The debt, aside from loans from European allies, consisted of paper that had been issued by the Continental Congress for soldiers' pay and bounties and army supplies. Almost all of it was now in the hands of Northern and European capitalists who had acquired it at cents on the dollar when it was "not worth a Continental." Jackson pointed out that there were not twenty of the original receivers of Continental paper left in Georgia and that soldiers had invariably been forced by necessity to sell their paper at a large discount. Hamilton's proposal was soon followed by another—the government should assume the remaining debts of the states, now also in the hands of speculators, and fund them in the same way. A proposal in the house to pay some of the proceeds to the original holders was roughly quashed by what was beginning to look like an organized party. Not only that, but, Jackson pointed out, certain money men who obviously had advanced knowledge of Hamilton's plans had been in Georgia very recently buying up debt certificates.

Mincing no words, Jackson called the speculators in the public debt "rapacious wolves" and "drone bees, sucking honey out of the hive, and affording no aid in its procurement."

Two types of republicanism and two different visions of the future were at the brink of serious conflict. A Massachusetts spokesman ridiculed the idea of paying off the original rather than the current holders of the debt—it would not give investors trust in "the full faith and credit" of the new government. Jackson replied: "Do not gentlemen think there is some danger on the other side? Will there not be grounds for uneasiness when the soldier and the meritorious citizen are called upon to pay the speculator more than ten times the amount they ever received from him for their securities?"

For Hamilton, allying the capital of the country and the government was a good and necessary move to guarantee stability, promote economic development, and strengthen the U.S. government at home and abroad. To others it looked an awful lot like the British system from which so much had recently been sacrificed to escape. In time Hamilton would propose a tariff to raise taxes from the consumers (incidentally arranging the tax on imported foreign goods so as to grant the internal market to "domestic industry"), a national bank (which was actually a private institution enjoying government powers and privileges), and a tax on whiskey distillers (which was heavy on the backcountry and the South but scarcely touched the Northeast). To a wary republican, the whole package constituted a way to drain wealth from the poor to the rich and from the producers of the South and West to the capitalists of New York and New England.

Jackson was nearly alone in 1790 in discerning and exposing the implications of what was afoot; he was joined only by William Maclay of Pennsylvania in the Senate. As one historian has put it:

> The astonishing thing is that the comparatively crude Maclay from the wilds of Pennsylvania and the leather-lunged James Jackson from sparsely settled Georgia should have caught the full significance of it all before it dawned on Jefferson and Madison.

A few years later Thomas Jefferson and James Madison would be organizing an opposition party to oppose Hamilton's "monarchical" schemes to stretch the "necessary and proper" clause of the Constitution past the breaking point, to replicate the British class and economic system in America, and to make the whole Union tributary to the capital of the Northeast. Jackson was way ahead of them.

Hamilton's friends pulled out all the stops to defeat Jackson for a second term as representative. His opponent was declared the winner, but Jackson proved that the election was corrupt and the House declared the seat vacant. Two years later Jackson was chosen as U.S. Senator. In the Senate he continued his vigorous fight against Secretary Hamilton's measures as they appeared. The tariff and the internal tax on whiskey would make the Southern States, which lived on exports, the "milch cow" of the Union. Jackson warned the Federalists that they could not milk the cow and ride it too. The whole of the Hamiltonian system was "odious, unequal, unjust, unnecessary" and promised that the "gnawing vulture [of taxation] whose appetite increases daily with what it feeds upon" would become perpetual. Hamilton's program, which was put forth as necessary to strengthen the Union, was actually having the opposite effect—it was alienating the people and raising sectional conflict.

James Jackson's greatest role as virtuous republican came with the Yazoo Claims, the first big financial scandal in America history, which became an international sensation.

A group of Philadelphia speculators, swearing each other to secrecy, formed a cabal with designs on Georgia's vast unsettled western lands—most of what was to become the states of Alabama and Mississippi. (The resulting affair was given the label "Yazoo," after the most valuable of the country in question, the rich lands between the Yazoo and Mississippi rivers.) In 1795 the Georgia legislature sold the Philadelphia conspirators 35 million acres of land for a little more than a penny an acre. This was the richest and most promising large piece of undeveloped real estate within the territory of the United States.

At the time the legislature made the deal, there were a number of men hovering about with pockets full of money to use where persuasion might be needed. These included James Wilson, arch-Federalist Justice of the U.S. Supreme Court, and one "Thomas Walsh," who was subsequently hanged on a different matter. You cannot keep a thing like that quiet, and public outrage in Georgia was loud. Learning of the affair while in Congress, Jackson wrote to a supporter at home: "I consider Georgia as having passed a confiscation act ... of your Children & mine, & unborn Generations, to supply the rapacious graspings of a few sharks . . . two-thirds of

Georgia will be held & owned by Residents in Philadelphia." The virtuous republican policy would be to sell the lands at modest prices to genuine settlers, providing a great social good and revenue for the state without taxation.

The public called on Jackson to come home and deal with the situation. He resigned his Senate seat after only two years and was received in Savannah with acclaim while the other Georgia Senator, who was implicated in the swindle, was burned in effigy. An angry new legislature was seated and Jackson managed the repeal of the deal made by the previous legislature. He was governor from 1798 to 1801, and while in that office he acted vigorously to prevent deeds being issued under the repealed 1795 act. In 1801 Jackson rejoined the Senate and served until his death in 1806 at forty-nine, his end probably hastened by the hardships endured as a soldier.

The Yazoo scandal had many complex ramifications and it remained a legislative and judicial issue into the 1830s before a sort of compromise was achieved, in the interest of plaintiffs who had (supposedly innocently) purchased from the original grantees of the lands. In the notorious case of *Fletcher v. Peck* in 1810, the U.S. Supreme Court invalidated Georgia's repeal of the Yazoo grant on the grounds that it violated the provision of the Constitution forbidding interference with the "sanctity of contracts." In other words, the Supreme Court ruled that private property rights, even if acquired corruptly, were superior to the will of the people and that state legislatures could be overruled by the federal court. The ruling did not settle the public controversy. John Randolph of Roanoke, another almost forgotten conservative voice of the early Union, continued to condemn the Yazoo corruption and usurpation for some years to come in Congress. Whatever the subject he was discussing, Randolph would pause, point a long bony finger at certain congressmen whom he considered complicit, and scream "Yazoo! Yazoo!"

On the question of immigration, James Jackson took a stand that latter-day conservatives should find sympathetic. When the first naturalization law was before the House, he argued for a long period of residence before the granting of citizenship. An immigrant himself, who had earned his American status the hard way, he did not want "the rank of American citizen" to become the world's plaything.

It was said that James Jackson left Congress no richer than he entered it. That is a high compliment and well worthy of imitation at any period of history.

There has long been a conventional understanding of American history that the soldiers of the War of Independence fought with the goal of establishing a new nation with a centralized national government. This was certainly true of Alexander Hamilton and John Marshall among others, at least judging by their postwar actions. However, the formulation is seriously misleading. The nationalists had a very hard sell and did not fully achieve their goal until Lincoln made it stick with massive warfare. There was another large group of soldiers who saw the goal of the Revolution as getting rid of the power of a centralized government to rule over Americans. They had a fellow-American *feeling* with comrades in other states for shared sacrifices, and they were willing to entertain a federal (not national) government to handle some of the joint affairs of the states, but they insisted that such a government must be kept within a strictly circumscribed role.

Such men were the real conservatives, for they wanted to preserve the essence of the Union that had emerged from the War of Independence, not transform it into something new. Many of the most important patriots of the Revolution held this view and gathered with Jefferson in support of it. To mention active soldiers of this persuasion, besides James Jackson of Georgia, these included Nicholas Gilman of New Hampshire, John Lansing of New York, Thomas Mifflin of Pennsylvania, John Francis Mercer of Maryland, Nathaniel Macon of North Carolina, Thomas Sumter of South Carolina, and James Monroe, St. George Tucker, and John Taylor of Virginia.

John Taylor of Caroline: Thomas Jefferson at Home

To explore the writings of John Taylor is, for a twenty-first-century American, an adventure like time travel or visiting a foreign country. It takes some time and effort to understand what is going on, but you return home with a greatly expanded perspective. You will acquire much forgotten wisdom in regard to such matters as constitutional government and political economy, which are of considerable value in an era of judicial activism and billion-dollar bank bailouts.

Thomas Jefferson testified in regard to his fellow Virginia planter and republican: "Col. Taylor and myself have rarely, if ever, differed in any political principle of importance. Every act of his life, and every word he ever wrote, satisfies me of this." It follows that anyone who wants to understand Thomas Jefferson's beliefs and what "Jeffersonian democracy" stood for should pay attention to the words that John Taylor wrote. Taylor was the systematic expositor of the political position that Jefferson represented in the public mind of his time and for several subsequent generations. In the public mind, Jefferson was not the *philosophe* celebrated or deplored by some later commentators, but the wise republican statesman who put the people before would-be elites and who had defeated the schemes of Alexander Hamilton, John Adams, and their friends, to concentrate too much power in the federal government. For his time and long after, Jefferson was less celebrated as the author of "all men are created equal," than as the author of "the principles of 1798," the Kentucky resolutions which had unequivocally declared the right of the sovereign people of a state to counter infringements of the Constitution by the federal government.

Jefferson's name has been invoked to endorse many different ideas and movements. As is the case with any revered figure in history, there are always those who want their agenda to be blessed by postmortem sponsorship. Jefferson lends himself to various uses because he was a cosmopolitan man of letters whose writings would be a treasure of his time, even if he had never led a political movement. But as a public man he understood that he was a representative of his society, not a philosopher whose speculations were to be enforced as divine wisdom. Also, he was a leader who needed to maintain a firm national majority and sometimes stated his principles in broad and conciliatory terms.

The real Jefferson emerges for anyone who will read his political papers and letters with an open mind, free of assumptions loaded on by later times. This real Jefferson was in sync with John Taylor, as he said. He opposed all unnecessary federal laws, taxes, expenditures, and debt; he believed that the sovereignty of the people was to be expressed through their states and that the federal government possessed no sovereignty at all; he deplored artificial privileges but believed in an aristocracy of talent; and he thought slavery to be an unfortunate problem, while strongly resenting any federal and Northern interference in the matter. Such was the Jeffersonian persuasion, the principles of which were laid out systematically and in depth by John Taylor of Caroline County, Virginia.

We can appreciate the deep conservatism of the Jeffersonian persuasion if we understand Russell Kirk's observation in *The Conservative Mind* that sometimes in telling American history "the acquisitive instinct" has been mistaken for "the conservative disposition." "Truly conservative statesmen," wrote Kirk, are "leaders whose chief desire is the preservation of the ancient values of society." Jeffersonians sought preservation of what to them was a largely satisfactory American society that had emerged from the colonial experience and the War of Independence—that indeed embodied some ancient British liberties that had been forgotten in the Mother Country. They opposed innovators and devotees of forced "progress," among whom Kirk cites Alexander Hamilton as a conspicuous example. In particular, Jeffersonians feared and opposed innovations that they believed would reconstruct society by putting the government in the service of "the acquisitive instinct." Such innovations were initiated by Hamilton, which would be revived again in the agendas of the Whig and Republican parties. This was the bedrock political program of Jeffersonian democracy, which Taylor in his writings crafted into a persuasive vision of truth and justice.

John Taylor was born in 1753 and died in 1824 at his plantation on the Rappahannock River between Richmond and Fredericksburg.

Like Jefferson, Taylor's father died when he was young but left him a rich inheritance of land and slaves. Like Jefferson he enjoyed the benefit of gifted mentors—in Taylor's case his uncle Edmund Pendleton, prominent among the Revolutionary leaders of Virginia. Like Jefferson, Taylor was educated at the College of William and Mary. Unlike the somewhat-older Jefferson, Taylor came of age at the outbreak of the War of Independence and saw much active military duty, characteristically refusing to accept pay and bounties for his patriotic service. He married a daughter of John Penn, a signer of the Declaration of Independence for North Carolina.

On three different occasions the Virginia General Assembly elected Taylor to fill out terms in the U.S. Senate, quite a compliment for one who did not seek and did not want office and in a state overflowing with talented statesmen. He left aside political office and a lucrative law practice to be a farmer, dedicated to improving the art and science of husbandry for those living on the land, whose interests he defended. For Taylor, a good farmer was more valuable to his fellow citizens than any number of politicians, judges, bankers, stock speculators, or military heroes.

Taylor's wisdom is contained in his books: *A Defense of the Measures of the Administration of Thomas Jefferson* (1804); *Arator: Being a Series of Agricultural Essays, Practical and Political* (1813); *Construction Construed, and Constitutions Vindicated* (1820); *Tyranny Unmasked* (1822); *New Views of the Constitution of the United States* (1823); and *An Inquiry into the Principles and Policy of the Government of the United States* (1814). The last, according to the magisterial American historian Charles A. Beard, "deserves to rank among the two or three really historic contributions to political science which have been produced in the United States."

Taylor's writing style has often been cited as an obstacle to his influence. His friend John Randolph of Roanoke reportedly said that Taylor's books would do much good if they could be translated into English. The criticism is a bit exaggerated. The style is conversational, that of a leisurely eighteenth century essayist or a farmer talking with his neighbors on the verandah. He communicates his understanding as one gentleman to another, with a good deal of humor and satire. Indeed humor is an effective way to confront the earnest political pundits and disingenuous centralizers of power who have motivated him to write. Referring to the advocates of a strong centralized government, Taylor wrote: "A crocodile has been worshipped, and its priesthood have asserted, that morality required the people to suffer themselves to be eaten by the crocodile." He is not an intellectual historian displaying his learning (which John Adams often seems). Rather than citing obscure bits of history or learned treatises, he refers to *Don Quixote*. If Sancho Panza had known about government bonds, he would have chosen them as his reward rather than the governorship of an island.

As the Constitutional scholar James McClellan has pointed out, Taylor's writings are a treasury of golden nuggets, such as this one, which is highly relevant to a time of almost immeasurably vast government debt:

> But an opinion that it is possible, for the present generation to seize and use the property of future generations, has produced to both the parties concerned, effects of the same complexion with the usual fruits of national errour [*sic*]. The present age is cajoled to tax and enslave itself, by the errour of believing that it taxes and enslaves future ages to enrich itself

A few other examples of homely political wisdom: "Inferior agents in all wicked plots suffer punishment in this world, whilst their leaders often avoid it until the next." "A power in a government of any form, to deal out wealth and poverty by law, overturns liberty universally; because it is a power by which a nation is infallibly corrupted." "A legislative power of regulating wealth and poverty, is a principle of such irresistible tendency, as to bring all political parties to the same standard."

Alexander Hamilton had made the preposterous assertion that "a public debt is a public blessing." Jefferson, when secretary of state, remembered an eye-opening event in which it became clear what this meant. At a supper, Vice-President John Adams remarked that the British Constitution, purged of its corruption, would be the best on earth. Secretary of the Treasury Alexander Hamilton quickly objected: no, it was its very corruption that gave the British government its stability, power, wealth, and energy. He meant that the public debt kept the rich and powerful united with the government by their stake in its interest-bearing bonds, and the availability of wealth gave the ministry ability to command obedient execution of its goals by the bestowal of patronage.

John Taylor was having none of this "paper and patronage aristocracy." Was this not what the War of Independence had been fought to break free of? Who was to pay for this but those who produced the real wealth of the country from the land, and who would become as burdened with taxes as the suffering masses of the Old World? And who was to profit except clever manipulators who produced nothing except paper and persiflage about the allegedly arcane mysteries of finance? Why indeed did the government, which had ample revenue from customs and public land sales, need to borrow at all, except to enrich the well-placed at no risk or effort to themselves? A closely related part of the Hamiltonian program was yet another swindle in the eyes of Jeffersonians: the National Bank perverted the Congress's constitutional duty to "regulate the currency," giving private parties the immensely profitable power to create money out of the air by printing paper. (This perspective is developed more fully in the essay on the economist Condy Raguet.)

Would not the people, by creating a stronger central authority, be paying for their own chains? And where did the Hamiltonians get the authority for their schemes? Virginia had agreed to no such thing when ratifying a written Constitution creating a government of specifically enumerated, limited, delegated powers. The Philadelphia Convention had voted down a proposal to give the Congress power to create corporations. Yet here was Hamilton arguing that it could do so because such a bank was "necessary and proper" in pursuit of delegated powers. In addition to exposing the bad policy involved, Taylor wrote of the Constitutional issue:

> To me this new notion of a constitution by implication is, I confess, exactly like no Constitution at all; nor has it been proved to my satisfaction, that principles ought to be lost in verbal definitions. . . . [Incorporating the Bank proposes] that an absolute sovereignty as to means does exist, where there is no sovereignty at all as to ends. . . . [Such a doctrine is] evidently inconsistent with the principle of dividing, limiting, balancing, and restraining political powers. . . . The habit of corrupting our political system by the instrumentality of inference, convenience and necessity, with an endless series of consequences attached to them, is the importer of contraband principles, and the bountiful grantor of powers not given, or withheld by our constitutions.

Elsewhere, Taylor refers to the drawing of "inferences" from plain language as "alchemy," "superstition," and "witchcraft." "Political words," he writes, "of all others are the most indefinite, on account of the constant struggle of power to enlarge itself" by ambitious construction of terms. A "phalanx of words" was being used by the Supreme Court to "distort the plainest provisions of the federal constitution."

All the Founders believed in republican government—a government resting on the consent of the people. Most also understood that such governments suffered from various defects that historically had almost always led to their downfall. The division between Jeffersonian conservatives and their opponents is to some extent represented by differing assessments of the source of danger. Jeffersonians feared "consolidation"—overweening and irresponsible power; the Federalists feared "disunion"—the loss of order, security, and prestige.

Hamilton had said that the people were a great beast—that human nature was flawed, that men were selfish and unreasonable and needed to be managed by their betters. Jefferson immediately had an irrefutable answer. "Where do these angels come from?" If men are flawed, where do you find these superior beings that are entitled to rule others? The remedy for human fallibility was not to empower some, but to make sure that power was as divided, limited, temporary, and as directly responsible to the people as possible.

Taylor's *Inquiry* is a reply to John Adams's *A Defense of the Constitutions of Government of the United States of America, Against the Attack of M. Turgot in his Letter to Dr. Price, Dated the Twenty-Second Day of March, 1778*. Adams shared the common European and Federalist assumption that unchecked majority rule would inevitably destroy society as the poor majority learned they could vote themselves the wealth of the rich minority. To his credit, Adams also recognized a different though related danger. The rich, powerful, wellborn, talented, and glamorous also posed a threat to the commonwealth through their ambitions and self-promotion—too often free governments had ended in the despotic rule of one man. Adams thought that Americans had invented the perfect cure for all these ills. The bicameral legislature, independent judiciary, and executive veto would guard again an unruly majority overstepping its rights. And the distinction and power of the upper house of the legislative body would contain and satisfy the ambitious who might otherwise undermine the state.

Again, Taylor was having none of it. Adams was creating artificial and useless political orders where they did not naturally exist. Such imagined "checks and balances" were no safeguard against the abuses of power. The obvious guard against usurpation of power was to divide and limit it as much as possible, which the American constitutions had done—by providing written, specific limits to the role of government in all of its branches. What was most to be guarded against was incremental stretching of those powers. Such stretching alone could legitimate the Hamiltonian program.

Further, wrote Taylor, John Adams was mistaken in his history. Good governments were not normally destroyed by the majority preying upon the wealth of the minority. For Taylor the lesson of history was the opposite. The guileless, unorganized majority of citizens went quietly about the business of earning their bread. They were not the perpetrators but the victims of bad government. The great mass of Europeans was impoverished by the exactions of their rulers, who held power over them for the benefit of a few. But the American population, providentially, was one of independent landowners, along with the merchants, artisans, and professional men who helped sustain agricultural society. The people had property and earnings to protect as well as the rich, and their greatest threat came from the government.

Governments became oppressive when a crafty minority managed to impose itself upon and live off the body of the society. In earlier times this had been done by force and superstition. Now it was to be done by fraud and mystification around words like "full faith and credit," "necessary and proper," "regulating the currency," and "protecting domestic industry." In Taylor's view:

> The useful and major part of mankind, comprised within natural interests (by which I mean agricultural commercial, mechanical, and scientifick; in opposition to legal and artificial, such as hierarchical, patrician, and banking) is exclusively the object of imposition, whenever words are converted into traitors to principles.

For Taylor, the important conflict was not between the rich and the poor but between the taxpayers and the tax consumers. This view long remained a basic way of understanding politics for American critics of Hamiltonian government. The idea still has potency. When Jeffersonians condemned "aristocrats," they meant people with artificial, unearned, government-granted privileges, not talented and honorable men who were the natural and necessary leaders of their communities.

John Adams or John Taylor? Who is the better historian, prophet, and guide for American conservatives?

To recover the Constitution as John Taylor understood and described it requires painstaking intellectual archeology. There is an astounding difference between that basic document and what we have now. Time, ambition, interest, ignorance, deception, misunderstanding, and the lust for power have covered it with layer upon layer of false assumptions and distorted postures.

The Constitution contains no reference to "nation" or "national." Indeed, Taylor observes that the emotional effect and un-reflected associations of "nation" were a major source of Constitutional usurpations and distortions. Throughout the Constitution, "United States" is a plural rather than the odd singular it later became. This plural was used in every law, treaty, proclamation, and public discussion from the beginning until well after Taylor's time. Americans sometimes spoke of the "nation" in recognition of a common identity, but their political connection was usually referred to as "the Union," i.e., the Union of the States.

The Declaration of Independence asserts that the thirteen colonies are, and of right ought to be, independent states. The Constitution announces itself to be *"For* the United States of America," not the "Constitution *of* the U.S." or the "U.S. Constitution." With this in mind, read the preamble which declares its purpose is to "form a more perfect Union" in order to "provide for the common defense" and "promote the general Welfare" (of the people of the states). In Article III, section 3, we learn that "Treason against the United States, shall consist only in levying War against *them,* or in adhering to *their* enemies."

To understand how Taylor saw the Constitution one must forget the iconic status of *The Federalist.* Those essays were a discussion of the Constitution as proposed, not the Constitution as ratified. They were polemics calculated to allay the fears of citizens of New York of a too centralized and irresponsible government (and not particularly successful arguments because ratification passed New York by the narrowest margin). Further, the authors, at least one of them, were obviously insincere. Immediately after securing ratification, Hamilton began to claim for the federal government powers that in *The Federalist* he had assured voters it did not possess. Besides, the political wisdom expressed in the essays were opinions—they were not the will of the people and had no official standing whatsoever.

Taylor's Constitution was not the proposal examined by *The Federalist* but the one ratified by the people of the states. It was to be interpreted in the light of the reservations stipulated in those ratifications; of the Ten Amendments, which had been promised as a condition of ratification and which reiterated the limited nature of the federal power; and of the Virginia and Kentucky resolutions of 1798-1800, which restated the sovereignty of the people of the states shortly before Jefferson and his friends assumed power. James Madison agreed, writing that the meaning of the Constitution is to be sought "not in the opinions or intentions of the body which planned and proposed it, but those in the State conventions where it received all the authority which it possesses."

Then and later it was denied that Jefferson had really endorsed state nullification of federal law, such as was adopted by South Carolina in 1832. One can only hold this position by ignoring the plain language of these documents. Jefferson, in his last year, and only two years before John C. Calhoun broached the right of nullification, privately recommended that Virginia should once more nullify federal legislation—the internal improvements expenditures that had stretched the powers to establish post roads and regulate interstate commerce into authority to subsidize private corporations to dig canals and construct roads.

Virginia at the time of the War of Independence had a history of five generations and almost two centuries with its own particular pride, identity, laws, and ways of life. Virginians considered their consent to the Constitution (ratification) as a policy to be decided by and for Virginians (in the same way they regarded slavery). The ratification was an act of the sovereign will of a specific people at a specific historical moment, not some vague, passive reception of saintly wisdom bestowed by "Founding Fathers" on an amorphous "people of the United States" who did not exist as a constitution-ratifying authority. The Virginia instrument of ratification stated that the sovereign's consent was not eternal but could be revoked when deemed necessary. Taylor's generation and the next several generations of Southerners understood what their fathers and grandfathers had intended in accepting the Constitution, even while the greatest economic and emotional force of the nineteenth century—nationalism—was gaining strength.

It is an often-stated fallacy that Taylor and those who asserted the states' rights position were advocates of "strict construction."

Taylor (and John C. Calhoun later) specifically rejected the idea that "strict construction" was a safeguard of the Constitution. The Constitution was not to be interpreted by judges, whatever their philosophy of "construction." No branch of the federal apparatus could be allowed the final judgment as to the limits of its own power. (Thus the later Borkian notion of "original intent," whereby judges adhere to the interpretations in earlier writings and previous court decisions rather than "adapting" the Constitution to new circumstances, is an irrelevant and illegitimate realm for Taylor.)

In our day, a "living Constitution" is one in which judges exercise the power to change the fundamental document by interpretation, in accordance with their ideas of changing times. Taylor's Constitution was one in which the people of the states were participants in an ongoing process of working out proper Constitutional interpretation. The Constitution was not a one-time opportunity which ever-after bound the people of the states to be passive, obedient recipients of whatever any branch of the federal government handed down. The meaning of the Constitution was to be determined by an active participation of the people of the states rather than by the arbitrary decrees of judges. Now that is a real "living Constitution"!

The combination of principles that Taylor represents may seem unfamiliar to twenty-first-century Americans, but it is very American and it long enjoyed widespread acceptance. On the one hand it was a conservative allegiance to the soil and those who labor in it and a defense of local community and inherited ways; on the other it was a populist suspicion of government and the maneuvers of capitalists, bureaucrats, and reformers. Taylor's writings are prophetic in portraying the downside of the course of history toward ever greater "consolidation." He foresaw the dominance of rent-seeking in the political process, judicial oligarchy, immense debt and burdensome taxation, unhealthy intrusion of the state into private society, and the concentration of wealth and power into fewer and fewer hands.

The Bayards of Delaware: America's Conservative Family

After witnessing the march of "progress" in the late nineteenth century, James A. Bayard, the younger, wrote, "We fancy that humanity is advancing because immense advances have been made in the physical sciences, but man the individual is the same impure being, the same creature of circumstance and mixture of good and evil as he has always been under varying types of civilization." In his estimation, universal suffrage and the push for human equality would end in the ruin of civilization:

> My conviction looking at past history of the world is, that nations die like men at different intervals of duration, and that what is called progress must be based on the moral culture of the people and not on merely intellectual excitement. . . . The whole doctrine of brining all men to equality in mental moral or physical endowments by so called education is simply an absurdity.

Equality, he argued, was impossible, for "Equality of civil rights may be and is rational, but equality is not the law of nature."

Bayard's assessment of human nature runs counter to the modern, dominant theory of universal egalitarianism. But he was from a family that personified American conservatism, and his statements fit that paradigm. They were a powerful and important clan. The Bayards were aristocratic, disinterested statesmen proud of their ancestral roots and impressive pedigree, but most importantly they were adherents to a cogent brand of conservatism that has virtually disappeared from contemporary American politics. Between 1804 and 1929, five members of the Bayard family served in the United States Senate. James A. Bayard, the elder, and his grandson, Thomas F. Bayard, Sr., played an important role in American foreign policy, and as such are the most conspicuous family members, but all five men were active at both the state and federal level throughout their lives. Yet, the Bayard family has been lost to time, possibly forgotten in part because their home state exceeds only Rhode Island in size, but more likely because their brand of conservatism does not mesh with progressive interpretations of American history.

Family

The Bayards (pronounced "by-erd") of Delaware are descended from the famous French knight, Chevalier de Bayard, "the knight without fear and beyond reproach." At his time of death, he chastised his former ally, Charles III, Duke of Bourbon, for "serving against your king, your country, and your oath." His chivalry and honor filtered through successive generations of the family. Several of the Bayard clan became Huguenots and settled in Holland to escape persecution. In the seventeenth century, Samuel Bayard married Anna Stuyvesant, the sister of the last Dutch governor of the New World colony New Netherland (New York), and after Samuel Bayard died in 1647, Anna and her four children sailed to the New World and landed in New Netherland in the spring of 1647. Her son, Petrus Bayard, became the patriarch of the Delaware Bayards.

Petrus joined the Labadist movement in 1684 and traveled with the church to a retreat called Bohemia Manor in Cecil County, Maryland, located on the 30,000-acre Bohemia Estate owned by Augustine Herman. When the Maryland Labadists dissolved the community in 1698, Petrus' son, Samuel Bayard, received a considerable portion of the estate. Samuel's son, James, married Mary Asheton of Virginia, and established the family at Bohemia Manor—what the Delaware Bayards often called their ancestral lands—in the early eighteenth century. James and Mary Bayard had two sons born at Bohemia Manor, John and James Asheton. John Bayard is well known to history as Col. John Bubenheim Bayard, the Revolutionary War hero. James Asheton Bayard's youngest son, James A. Bayard, the elder, would become the first of the Bayards to settle in Delaware and the first of the clan to hold a seat in the United States Senate.

The Bayards of Delaware were all impressive men who moved easily in society. James A. Bayard, the elder, settled in Wilmington in 1787 and quickly introduced himself to the best families in the state: the Rodneys, Ridgelys, Claytons, Bassetts, Reads, and Wells. These families, along with the DuPonts, formed the basis of several solid political and personal friendships for the Bayards in later years. Contemporaries described the Bayard men as hedonistic.

They drank heavily, smoked cigars, gambled, and participated in the balls, hunts, sailing trips, summer vacations, and picnics of Delaware society. Women enjoyed their company, and all were well educated, impeccably dressed, well spoken and mannered, and athletic. Only John Quincy Adams spoke disparagingly of James A. Bayard, the elder (and it was said Bayard the elder could find friendship with anyone). James A. Bayard, the elder; his son, Richard H. Bayard; and his grandson, Thomas F. Bayard, Sr., were popular in both European and American society. Their private correspondence also reveals that they were affectionate husbands and fathers, and James A. Bayard; the younger, was classified as one of the best Biblical scholars in Wilmington. Like their ancestor the Chevalier Bayard, they considered honor to be the highest personal quality. James A. Bayard, the elder, even dueled to protect his.

James A. Bayard, the elder, married Ann Bassett in 1795, daughter of Richard Bassett, who was the first United States Senator from Delaware and heir to Augustine Herman's Bohemia Estate. Bayard served as the Delaware member of the House of Representatives from 1797-1803, and later in the United States Senate from 1804-13. He was the only Federalist appointed by the James Madison administration to the Peace Commission during the War of 1812, and he ultimately helped broker the Treaty of Ghent that ended the war. His sons, Richard H. Bayard and James A. Bayard, the younger, followed their father to the Senate. Richard Bayard also served as Chief Justice of Delaware and *chargé d'affaires* to Belgium. James A. Bayard, the younger, held his seat in the Senate during the tumultuous 1850s and was one of the few senatorial voices opposed to both the War Between the States and military Reconstruction. He was considered for president in 1860, 1864, and 1872 and was elected speaker of the Southern Democratic delegation in 1860 after they bolted the Charleston Convention.

Thomas F. Bayard, Sr., James A. Bayard's son, assumed his father's seat in the United States Senate in 1869, and like his father, was recognized as a leading conservative voice and a staunch opponent of Reconstruction. He was considered for president in 1880 and 1884 and accepted the position of secretary of state in the first Grover Cleveland administration in 1885. When Cleveland returned to office in 1893, Bayard was appointed ambassador to Great Britain, the first American to hold that title, and he served until 1897. His son, Thomas F. Bayard, Jr., was the first Bayard elected to the Senate through the popular vote. He took his seat in 1923, served one term, and was the last Bayard to hold an elected position in the federal government.

Statesmen

When the 1800 presidential election ended in an Electoral College deadlock between Thomas Jefferson and Aaron Burr, Federalists had the perfect opportunity to destroy the potential presidency of their arch-political rival Jefferson. As per the Constitution, the election would be thrown to the House of Representatives, a body the Federalists controlled, and thus the Federalists mulled the possibility of throwing the election to Burr. James A. Bayard, the elder, was the lone representative from Delaware during this critical juncture in American history, and because the vote in the House was by state, Bayard wielded considerable power. He was a Federalist and a John Adams supporter, but he was a man with an independent character who did not display the same level of partisanship as other Federalists of his era.

Alexander Hamilton famously wrote to several prominent Federalists attempting to convince them that Jefferson would be the preferable choice over Burr, a man whom Hamilton believed no one could trust. Bayard tended to agree, but the political revolution of 1800 worried him. He believed in the sovereignty of the people and supported the popular will through election, but he wanted assurances that Federalists would continue to be represented in the new administration and thought Jefferson would take political revenge on the Federalists. What transpired has become the subject of considerable historical debate (Jefferson called Bayard a liar in his diary while Bayard's sons twice came to his defense through the press and later in the United States Senate).

Bayard met with a Jefferson ally, John Nicholas, during the contested election in the House of Representatives. Nicholas relayed that Jefferson would not remove several Federalist appointees in the federal government; with that guarantee, Bayard determined to cast a blank vote in the election and help swing other states in Jefferson's favor, an action that resulted in Jefferson's election on the thirty-sixth ballot. This move did not endear him to stalwart Federalists in the North, but it displayed Bayard's willingness to act in the spirit of the Constitution. Bayard suggested in private correspondence that he would rather have Jefferson as president than disunion, a position New England Federalists appeared unwilling to adopt. To Bayard, Jefferson's election represented the spirit of compromise that formed the Union.

Shortly thereafter, Bayard declined an appointment by Pres. John Adams as minister to France. His reasoning exemplifies the statesmanship of the entire family. The post carried a salary of $18,000, a substantial sum for the period, and Bayard would have ultimately served at the pleasure of the Jefferson administration. Bayard thought that because he led the congressional effort to have Jefferson elected, opponents could accuse him of impropriety, so he determined to retain his seat in congress rather than serve under a cloud of ethical misconduct. As he said in a letter to his cousin: "My ambition shall never be gratified at the expense of a suspicion. I shall never lose sight of the motto of the great Origonal of our name." He was later the political target of Delaware Republicans and lost his seat in the House of Representatives by fifteen votes to his close friend Caesar A. Rodney, a man whom Bayard said was more "peopletick" than himself. He was elected to the United States Senate by the Delaware Legislature in 1804.

The Bayard men were often in the minority in the Senate, and in many instances held unpopular opinions, but as statesmen, they charted a course based on principle and the rule of law, what Russell Kirk once termed "custom, convention, constitution, and prescription." As James A. Bayard, the elder, wrote shortly after his defeat in 1802, "I am persuaded that the people cannot be reasoned out of their folly and that they must be left to *feel* the evils now generating, before they will open their ears to anything said against their present opinions." His son, James A. Bayard, the younger, echoed this sentiment during his long opposition to the War Between the States. In 1863, Bayard said:

> The truth will out, ultimately . . . I never mean to make any question here except a question which I believe is vital in principle; but when I do make those questions I have no fears—though they may be voted down by the majority of the hour, though they may not be known at first—that great truths will not triumph, with a little energy and a little perseverance.

And in 1896, Henry St. George Tucker of Virginia described Thomas F. Bayard, Sr., as the "one sympathetic voice amid the roar of unbridled passion" during the "dark days" of Reconstruction.

Tucker said Bayard "stepped into the arena almost singlehanded, and alone and cheerfully accepted the gage of battle in behalf of a brave but friendless people."

Because all but one of the Bayard men served in the Senate before the adoption of the Seventeenth Amendment, they retained a disinterested view of politics. James A. Bayard, the younger, remarked in 1869 that he was proud that "so many generations of our family have been represented in the Senate with neither fortune, landed interest, or solicitation to obtain the position." Though considered the best candidate for president on the Democrat ticket in 1884, Thomas F. Bayard, Sr. refused to campaign for his own nomination—as did his father and grandfather—and said of his Senatorial career, "I am an opponent of the entire system which turns public offices into mere rewards for partizan services, and results in the creation of a brood of tricky and evasive politicians, where conscientious statesmen should be found." Six years later, Bayard declared that:

> Unhappy is that nation from whose people is banished a belief in the disinterestedness of public service, which is naturally accompanied by broad and liberal views, which do not measure or test great purposes by constant reference to one small object—personal advantage or profit. This it is that makes mercenary politicians such unsafe leaders, and causes national interests so often to be led to their destruction by men of narrow understandings, incapable of taking any but mercenary and commercial views of questions of governmental policy.

Like the republicans in the founding generation, these men believed they were above petty partisanship and narrow interests but lamented that the course of American history was against them. The "political traders," as James A. Bayard, the younger, described them, would, he believed, destroy self-government and force the best men from public life. "The imperial government of France," he thundered in 1869, "with its six million majority, affords ample illustration of the inefficiency of such a remedy [universal suffrage and professional politicians] to secure liberty against the aggressions of power." History has proven him correct, and the Bayard family ultimately retired from federal service, swept out by the wave of public sentiment and demagoguery the Bayards had long resisted.

War, Peace, and Empire

In June 1812, James A. Bayard, the elder, rose in opposition to a proposed declaration of war against Great Britain. He offered one of the few speeches against the war, and it was circulated across the country as the best argument against rushing haphazardly into conflict. Bayard was not opposed to war in principle—he had supported potential hostilities against Great Britain in 1806 and 1807 and against France numerous times—but he could not concede to war at this juncture. His position was simple: "If we are to come out of the war, as we enter into it, after having wasted the blood and treasure of the nation, and loaded the country with debt and taxes, it would certainly be more rational to submit at once to the wrongs we endure. If we expect to extort any concession from Britain, we must be prepared for a long, obstinate, and bloody conflict." The United States army and navy, in his estimation, would be easily defeated by a more powerful foe, and he asked, "In peace, we require no defense, and shall we declare war in order to defend ourselves?" His arguments were in vain. The United States Congress declared war on Great Britain one day after his speech.

One year later, Pres. James Madison appointed Bayard to serve on the peace commission charged with ending the war in an agreeable manner for the United States. During negotiations, the British were cold, intractable, and demanded subjugation, but after the British army burned Washington, D.C. in 1814, Bayard believed public opinion had swayed to support prolonging what had become a defensive conflict for American rights. A string of victories buttressed his claim, and the Treaty of Ghent, signed on 24 December 1814, solidified American independence. History proved Bayard correct that the war could have been avoided and that the United States was initially ill-prepared to fight. His opposition was a fine example of conservative resistance to war. Rather than rush headlong into a disaster, Bayard urged Americans to postpone hostilities in order to equip and train an army and navy and to give diplomacy time to bear fruit. Blood lust had never been the traditional American foreign policy.

His son, James A. Bayard, the younger, faced similar circumstances in 1861. The American public had become excited over the secession of seven Southern States, and the drum-beat of war began to echo across the North. Bayard became one of the lone voices against what he called a "fanatical" war of "subjugation" and "extermination," and his arguments mirrored those of his father fifty years earlier.

In March 1861, one month prior to the firing on Fort Sumter, Bayard spoke for three days on the Senate floor in opposition to a potential war against the South. He offered a resolution in the name of "humanity and the principle avowed in the Declaration of Independence" that would have allowed President Lincoln, with the advice and consent of the Senate, to negotiate a treaty of separation between the United States and the Confederate States. Bayard cautioned that if war was the outcome of secession, "This would be no short war." Southern men, he surmised, would "fight for their homes and firesides as they will not fight for conquest, and will endure the utmost extent of privation and suffering rather than yield to the invader, and disparity of force never insures the conquest of an invaded country." Peace, he argued, was the only way to preserve civil government, liberty, and the Union of the Founding Fathers. "Have we not the right," he asked, "has this Government the power, to accept that declaration; not to destroy the Union, but to preserve it, and maintain peace with those States?" In a later speech, he stated, "I confess, that when I think of the blood that must flow in this contest, this unnatural contest, of the devastation that must ensue, of the human lives that must be sacrificed, a shudder runs though my frame and my heart sickens with despair."

When his son-in-law joined the Union army in October 1861, Bayard pressed his case for peace more firmly in his private correspondence. He wrote:

> In embarking on this war therefore, you enlist in a war for invasion of another people. If successful it will devastate if not exterminate the Southern people and this is miscalled Union. If unsuccessful then peaceful separation must be the result after myriads of lives have been sacrificed, thousands of homes made desolate, and property depreciated to an incalculable extent. . . . Why in the name of humanity can we not let those States go?

Humanity consistently drove Bayard to argue against the horrors of war, particularly in a case where he believed rational diplomacy could have saved hundreds of thousands of lives. Bayard concluded the Republican Party was bent on war before the first shots were fired, and that their motivation was hardly humane:

> Their intent is the devastation and obliteration of the Southern people as the means of retaining power, and yet I doubt that the history of the world has ever, with the exception of the French reign

of terror, shown so imbecile, so corrupt, and so vindictive rulers over any people as those with which this country is now cursed.

The War would not conserve anything and was in Bayard's opinion the antithesis of the founding tradition, a tradition he relentlessly fought to preserve.

When his son, Thomas F. Bayard, Sr., assumed the duties of United States Secretary of State in 1885, the course of American imperialism blazed by political centralization had already become entrenched in the American consciousness. But Bayard never accepted the premise of American "Manifest Destiny," and though he pressed American interests, he resisted the colonial impulse of the late nineteenth century. Bayard's approach was of peaceful commercial exchange, freedom of the seas, and the desire to keep small, independent republics free from the grasp of European powers. In 1893, Bayard wrote that, "Our great Republic will perish if we embark upon an Imperial system of acquisition of outlying dependencies" and in 1895, after discussing the impact of "consolidation of empire," the "autocratic hand of power," and the "destructive forces of warfare" on world politics, he asked, "Where is the safety and personal freedom of the individual?"

In Bayard's mind, imperialism not only limited individual liberty but the liberty of sovereign nations. For example, Bayard supported the "Monroe Doctrine," but bristled at attempts to use it as a means to establish "protectorates" over Latin American states. He concurred with John Bassett Moore's argument that:

> Our position is not that of an involuntary military force, at the beck and call of any American state that may stand in need of it. . . . We have not assumed to forbid European powers to settle their quarrels with American states by the use of force any more than we have hesitated to do so ourselves. . . . The suggestion has lately been made in various quarters that it is a violation of the Monroe Doctrine for a European power to employ force against an American republic for the purpose of collecting a debt or satisfying a pecuniary demand. . . . There is nothing in President Monroe's declarations even remotely touching this subject.

Bayard could not countenance placing American sovereignty in the hands of Latin American politicians, a group he deeply distrusted. He declared to Pres. Grover Cleveland in 1895, "For the United States to place in the control of such a set of men the virtual control of peace and war with European powers, would be simple madness. . . . When our countrymen comprehend the consequences of committing our National welfare to the virtual control of South and Central American politicians and jobbers, they will recoil aghast."

Like his father and grandfather and unlike the Eastern imperialists led by Theodore Roosevelt, Bayard believed the best course for the United States and for American liberty was to avoid war, press for peace, and maintain American freedom of action. Imperialism and war could never secure those goals. The Bayard's foreign policy illustrates that American conservatism was often the home of peaceful men opposed to military adventurism and the resulting consolidation and destruction of individual freedom it produced. They also believed that war should only be pursued in extreme circumstances and must be weighed against the blood, money, and resources expended in the process.

Federalism

Like other Federalists of his day, James A. Bayard, the elder, viewed federal authority as a check on what Founding Father Elbridge Gerry called the "evils of democracy." He thought the Constitution offered a hedge against popular excitement and political novelties, such as universal egalitarianism. He explained to his father-in-law in 1798 that the French Revolution, "scattered sentiments thro' the world as powerful and destructive as the swords of the Goths and vandals [which destroyed the Roman Empire]." Later, he remarked that the French Revolution created a "storm" which the people of France sought to "drive over Europe," but was now ready to "break upon her own head." The only refuge appeared to be monarchy, though he thought it could not be "re-established without deluging the country with blood. And yet the nation must cast a longing eye to some port which can shelter them from the perpetual tempest of Jacobinism." This did not make Bayard a monarchist. He simply feared the effects of "Jacobinism" on society and government.

As such, he consistently defended delegated federal authority, but he viewed the United States as a *federal* republic, not a consolidated nation. In 1803, Bayard stated, "I believe as the United States *are* one great commercial Republic," [emphasis added] and he called the Constitution a "federal compact." Bayard also believed that the size of his home state necessitated supporting the Constitution. In a letter to John Adams after the 1800 election, Bayard wrote that because Delaware lacked "resources which could furnish the means of self protection . . . [he] was compelled [to vote for Jefferson] by the obligation of a sacred duty so to act as not to hazard the constitution upon which the political existence of the State depends." His federalism was born both from his public station and his view that Delaware could not survive as an independent state.

His son, James A. Bayard, the younger, made clear his positions on federalism in an 1833 treatise on the Constitution entitled *A Brief Exposition of the Constitution of the United States*. He stated that, "The government of the United States can claim no powers which are not granted to it by the Constitution, either in express terms or by necessary implication," and, "It is, no doubt, a government of limited powers; and can exercise no authority not delegated by the Constitution." He considered the states sovereign, "except so far as they are controlled or modified by the Constitution of the United States." Bayard displayed a type of federalism not unlike many of the "mild federalists" of the founding period. He supported the Constitution and a stronger central government but insisted that states retained powers not delegated to the federal government, and by the eve of war in 1861, he argued state authority served as a check on unconstitutional federal power.

The Republicans in 1861, he suggested, wanted to "make numbers alone the measure of political power, disregarding State sovereignty and the mixed character which our ancestors impressed upon this Federal Republic." The "Federal Republic" of the founders was created by the States, and he contended that "the words, 'We the people of the United States', mean nothing more than We, the several people of the States hereby united." Thus, the states "yielded, delegated, or ceded . . . a portion of their sovereignty to a common Government for the mutual protection and benefit of the people of each and all." But this did not mean that the states became subordinate to the will of the federal government or of simple majorities, and he believed both the War Between the States and later military Reconstruction destroyed the Union of the Founders. In 1867, Bayard argued that Republican legislation was "utterly subversive of the semblance of free government [and would end] in one of . . . two alternatives—either a concentrated, consolidated bureaucratic despotism or anarchy." Later, he said, "I am also opposed to the consolidation of all powers in a single government, and believe that the amendment now proposed [fifteenth Amendment] removes the last barrier which secures the States a single right against the Federal Government."

By the time of his death in 1880, Bayard believed the Union of the Founders was long dead, replaced by a consolidated government inconsistent with liberty and the original intentions of the Constitution. He wrote in 1833 that, "as we value our liberty and independence, we should cherish the Union, recollecting, that upon its preservation, depends the dignity, safety, and happiness of our country." Of course by Union, he meant the federal republic of the Founders, a Union his father fought to preserve in the 1800 election and he defended in vain on the Senate floor during the 1860s. His words did not apply to the Union that the Republicans created in the decades after the War Between the States.

Thomas F. Bayard, Sr., replaced his father in the Senate in 1869 and immediately took a prominent role in defending states' rights and limited federalism. Bayard was one of a handful of senators who openly challenged the Republican Party and radical Reconstruction. Like his father, Bayard opposed the Fifteenth Amendment to the Constitution, not out of racism, but because it was a "direct, open, flagrant violation of the spirit and letter of the fundamental law of this country that we have all sworn to sustain." Most importantly, Bayard saw the amendment as an attempt to perpetuate the Republican majority, crush political opposition, and centralize power in Washington:

> That power you propose to take from the Sates and deposit with the Federal Government; to consolidate the power of all powers, that which underlies and creates all other powers; and that you propose to place in the hands of Congress. . . . It is the intention by a measure like this to destroy first all shadow of freedom in the exercise of their opinion by the people of these three States[Mississippi, Texas, and Virginia which had to conditionally ratify the amendment to "re-enter" the Union]; and next, having destroyed that, to make their votes the instrument whereby you crush out the sentiment of the northern States.

Bayard kept applying the rhetorical pressure. In 1870, he stated,

> The Honorable Senator declares . . . that that which was a republican form of government in 1787 is not such in 1870; that the lapse of time, the changes in the condition of the country have destroyed the

definition and signification of these words which are older than the language in which we speak.

He asked his Republican colleagues to define a republic and wondered if Delaware met their definition:

> Delaware, a republican State before the United States had existed as a Government; that was a republic long before you had your confederation of republics; and forsooth, if this doctrine is to be attempted, then we shall have—what? We shall have the States that made this Union—the creators of the Union—converted into mere creatures, to be molded and turned as language shall find itself more conveniently used by an accidental majority of Congress.

He finished in a thundering denunciation of political centralization:

> What bald humbugs and wretched shams are your reconstructed governments and your "resuscitated States," as they have been termed in the course of this debate! What honest man but must laugh in scorn at these specimens Radical manufacture, set up here as republican States! They are the creations of violence and revolution, based upon the denial of every underlying principle of our original government.

Bayard recognized that the Republican Party killed the Union of the Founders and buried the Constitution. The states could no longer resist the central government, and by "Radical manufacture" they had been recreated as simple provinces of the central government. In 1872, Bayard urged his fellow Democrats to resist Republican usurpations of power and control of the states: "Give us a free Federal election, an election undisturbed by Federal money, by Federal threats, by Federal officials, by Federal bayonets; unchain the great heart of the American people, and let them vote freely."

Three years after he retired from public service, James A. Bayard, the younger, surveyed the political landscape and found little to appreciate:

> I am however but a "looker on in Vienna" now, but I fancy that I can foresee ultimate results more clearly than many of the actors. There are other matters such as the increase of large cities and their relative control over the rural population with the vice of universal suffrage controlled by the common government and the democratization of the Bar and the Press which make me anything but sanguine as to our future.

Furthermore, he had "no faith in the self-government of dense urban masses, for individual character is lost in the crowd until a Cromwell or Napoleon comes." He had the year prior blamed the political turbulence of the 1860s and 1870s on "the Yankee school system. It may stimulate the brain but it ignores man's moral nature and produces discontent with their condition among the masses. . . . God help the country in which the masses are merely stimulated and trained to act in combinations which are always, sooner or later, controlled by demagogues."

His melancholy assessment of the future was, in many ways, spot on. The United States is saturated with demagoguery; urban areas have often times over-run rural areas at the polls; public men have enriched themselves with the trappings of office; the states have become subservient to the central authority to an incalculable extent; the evils of democracy have often forced the best men from public life; and the problems of war are often ignored by blood thirsty politicians bent on enhancing their reputation for posterity. Throughout their public careers, the Bayard men resolutely maintained an attachment to limited federalism, a distrust of uncontrolled central power, and a reliance on principled statesmanship to challenge perceived abuses of power. They understood the history of Western Civilization and were proud that their ancestry had served with distinction through many tumultuous events. They should be often studied and emulated.

James Fenimore Cooper: The Aristocrat as Democrat

James Fenimore Cooper (1789-1851) is one of the great pioneer figures of American literature. He will always be best known as the creator of the "Deerslayer," a prototype of the American Western hero that remains powerful to this day. "Natty Bumppo," hero of *The Last of the Mohicans, The Deerslayer,* and other novels, was an ideal American—a courageous fighter, master of the wilderness beyond civilization, a deadeye shot, plain-spoken, and a model of simple honesty and integrity. Cooper's frontier books, along with his novels about the War of Independence (like *The Pilot* and *The Spy*), and his histories of real American naval exploits, contributed greatly to the building of national pride and identity.

Less known about Cooper is that in his book *The American Democrat* (1838) and his "novels of manners" about the transformation of New York State society in the early nineteenth century, he was a perceptive chronicler and critic of some of the less admirable characteristics of American democracy that he saw developing. What Cooper deplored has so long been commonplace that Americans are scarcely aware that there was once a different version of liberty and democracy.

The American Democrat, along with the works of John Taylor of Caroline and John C. Calhoun, is one of the most important and original political treatises written in the antebellum United States. The book has been admired by later commentators, among them H. L. Mencken and Robert Nisbet. Mencken, who was notoriously disdainful of Cooper's fiction, wrote, nearly a century after its publication, that in *The American Democrat* Cooper was "the first American to write about Americans in a really fresh spirit" and that "his prophecies were as sound as his observations were accurate."

Cooper thought that the direction taken by American democracy in his time was subverting the spirit and conditions of independence and liberty that had been expressed and established by the War of

Independence. Majority rule, a good thing in itself, was becoming a vague but imperative public opinion. "'They say,'" Cooper wrote, "is the monarch of this country." "Publick opinion" was not the will of the people but an artificial thing produced by designing men with hidden agendas, making use of political party organizations and shameless newspapers. It was amorphous, irresponsible, and highly manipulable. It rode roughshod over individual rights and legal principles. It was, Cooper believed, usurping the proper authority of lawful majority rule. It could even be manipulated by foreign governments, something with which later Americans are all too familiar.

"It is a besetting vice of democracies," Cooper wrote, "to substitute publick opinion for law. This is the usual form in which masses of men exhibit their tyranny. . . . The disposition of all power is to abuses, nor does it at all matter that its possessors are a majority." Further, the supposed will of the people was not only dominating government, it had begun to interfere in things that were none of its business—manners, private life and property, and legal principles. Independence of mind and character were giving way to conformity and mediocrity in every sphere of life.

Cooper's perception of the direction of American society in the 1830s and 1840s is similar to that of his contemporary, Alexis de Tocqueville, generally recognized as the most insightful foreign observer of America in the nineteenth century. Tocqueville admired America and democracy but he also noted the vapid conformity of thinking and lack of independent minds that he found. Alexander Solzhenitsyn, a brilliant foreign observer of twentieth-century America, described the same condition, observing that Americans had wide freedom of expression but that all the newspapers said exactly the same thing.

Cooper observed that good men were no longer expressing their true opinions except in private.

> The man who would dare to resist a monarch, shrinks from opposing an entire community. . . . The neighbours!—What a contemptible being a man becomes, who lives in constant dread of the comments and judgments of these social supervisors! and what a wretch the habit of deferring to no principle better than their decision has made many a being . . . by the *surveillance* of ignorance, envy, vulgarity, gossipping, and lying! . . . . the man who yields to such a government exhibits the picture of a giant held in bondage by a pigmy.

Before the War of Independence, New York State beyond the Hudson River Valley was unsettled wilderness still dominated by powerful Indian nations. Cooper's father, William, was one of the dynamic figures in the development of the region west of Albany after the Revolution, and Cooper grew up in an area in the process of settlement. Except for study at Yale (which he entered at age fourteen), a stint in the Navy as a young man, and a long trip to Europe (which doubtless influenced his perspective on America), J. F. Cooper spent his life around Cooperstown, founded by his father at the headwaters of the Susquehanna River on Lake Otsego.

Cooper's region not only developed from wilderness to settled land during his lifetime, it underwent a demographic change that altered his state's society and culture. New York State received an overflow of people from crowded and infertile New England. By the end of Cooper's life, a large majority of the New York population was of this origin. The old Anglo-Dutch society of the New York colony was quite different from that of the "Yankees" of New England. The ethnic term "Yankee," in fact, originated among New Yorkers. Before the War Between the States, the term everywhere referred specifically to New Englanders, whether at home or in the particular areas further west where they were settlers. The name was not particularly complimentary, suggesting sharp trading and religious intolerance and hypocrisy.

York State society was unique, but it resembled the South more than it did New England. The transformation of this society by "Yankees" is vividly chronicled by Cooper in his "Littlepage" trilogy—*Satanstoe, The Chainbearer,* and *The Redskins*—and in his Effingham novels, *Homeward Bound* and *Home as Found,* published between 1838 and 1846. The conflict of Yankee and Yorker is the main theme of these works. (The other great early American writer from New York, Washington Irving, also used this theme. Remember the encounter between Ichabod Crane from Connecticut and the Hudson Valley Dutch in "The Legend of Sleepy Hollow"?) It was the "Yankees" who brought to New York, and then to the rest of the North, the changes that Cooper deplored. Their bad influence on society was the base for the bad influence in politics.

Cooper believed that the natural leadership of American democracy came from landed families of established public service and patriotism, such as had largely carried through the War of Independence. An aristocracy in society was not a contradiction to democracy but rather a necessity for it to function at its best. "The tendency of democracies is, in all things, to mediocrity. . . . This circumstance . . . renders the introduction of a high standard difficult." Literature, arts, architecture, manners, and public and private ethics tended to fall to a common mediocre level. Equality before the law by no means required social equality. "Equality of condition is incompatible with civilisation," Cooper wrote. In America there was an equality of rights, giving everyone the legal status that had been possessed only by the privileged few in the Old World. However, Cooper noted:

> The rights of property being an indispensable condition of civilisation, and its quiet possession everywhere guaranteed, equality of condition is rendered impossible. . . . Equality of condition is nowhere laid down as a governing principle of the institutions of the United States, neither the word, nor any inference that can be fairly deduced from its meaning, occurring in the constitution.

Nor was it laid out in the state constitutions.

From the 1830s onward Cooper found himself confronted in both the public and the private spheres with pushy newcomers. They were men without respect for law and tradition except as served their own interest, who were manipulating government for personal profit, and who proclaimed the authority of the supposed will of the majority to interfere with private rights and activities.

Two incidents, as unfriendly critics have noted, were significant for Cooper. There was a lovely peninsula on Lake Otsego which Cooper and his father had freely allowed the community to use for fishing, boating, and picnicking. When he returned from Europe in 1833, Cooper found that the locals presumed to be entitled to do with this land whatever they wished. When Cooper objected, this private matter became a newspaper uproar in which he was attacked by Whig party editors as a cruel, grasping aristocrat—an enemy of the people.

Second in Cooper's experience were the "anti-rent riots" which were marked by considerable violence in some sections of New York over a period of several years. Large land grants had been made to certain families under the Dutch rule of New Amsterdam, something that was commonplace in the English colonies as well. Cooper's wife belonged to such a family. These "patroon" families had leased land to a great many farmers. The details are varied and complicated, but generally the tenants had been given very-long-term leases with no rent in the early years and mild rents thereafter, and the "patroons" had provided infrastructure. For the owners it was a way to build wealth for their family's future as the land gained value and to contribute to the growth of the country. For the tenants it was a good living, superior to what would have been involved in buying land. That was, until a serious attempt was made to collect rents.

In the late 1830s and early 1840s, "anti-rent" became a political and vigilante movement. It was asserted that the farmers were the rightful owners of the lands they had leased and that the original owners were aristocratic tyrants perpetuating a feudal system. The renters' position was presented not only as a matter of justice but as imperative and irrefutable, because it was the will of the people and because it was based on the equality that was necessary for democracy. For Cooper, this meant that designing rogues had got up an unjust cause in which "democracy" was made to interfere with individual rights and the law by denouncing what were ordinary private business arrangements as tyranny. This was not, in his view, what democracy was all about. It represented a perversion in the spirit of democracy arising out of the aggression, defective character, and wrong principles of "Yankees." Democracy was no longer a matter of liberty under law but had become a matter of power and appetite.

"Democracy" was coming to mean that people had a right to whatever they happened to want, the law and private rights be damned. Cooper wrote that "a state of society which pretends to the protection that belongs to civilisation, and fails to give it, only makes the condition of the honest portion of the community so much the worse, by depriving it of the protection conferred by nature, without supplying the substitute." Because power came from "the people," politicians were pretending that it had no limits and that their own self-serving interests were the will of the people. "He who would be a courtier under a king, is almost certain to be a demagogue in a democracy," Cooper wrote. In both cases, the ruler was being cleverly flattered for the benefit of the courtier.

The appropriately named character "Jason Newcome" from Connecticut is portrayed in the Littlepage trilogy as the personification of the "democratic" revolution in New York society and politics:

Jason had a liberal supply of Puritanical notions, which, were bred in-and-in in his moral and, I had almost said, in his physical system . . . this man had strong points about him, and a native shrewdness that would have told much more in his favour had it not been accompanied by a certain evasiveness of manner, that caused one constantly to suspect his sincerity, and which often induced those who were accustomed to him to imagine he had a sneaking propensity that rendered him habitually hypocritical. Jason held New York in great contempt, a feeling he was not always disposed to conceal, and of necessity his comparisons were usually made with the state of things in Connecticut, and much to the advantage of the latter.

However, Jason did admire the rising class of newly rich men in New York City, "for he never failed to defer to money, come in what shape it would. It was the only source of human distinction that he could clearly comprehend." Jason was certainly hard-working and entrepreneurial. He managed to get control (often clandestinely) of many of the essential businesses of the community—the tavern, store, and lumber and grist mills—and to get whatever local office he wanted. Cooper vividly describes how the rising and astute politician Newcome pre-managed and packed a supposedly open citizens' meeting to give the imprimatur of "publick opinion" to his agenda. Jason, a Cooper character observes, "was a leading politician, a patriot by trade, and a remarkable and steady advocate of the rights of the people, even to minutiae. Those who know mankind will not be surprised . . . to hear it added that he was a remarkable rogue in the bargain."

The Yankees' depredations upon society and manners were as bothersome to Cooper as their depredations upon politics and economy. They were pushy social climbers, insisting that their betters treat them as equals, but refusing to grant the same to those who were less successful and prosperous. Jason presumed an intimate friendship with mere acquaintances and "insisted to the last that he *knew* every gentleman in the county, whom he had been accustomed to hear alluded to in discourse." He was so officiously over-intimate with a lady, that she had to tell him in refusing his ministrations: "When I go to Connecticut, I shall feel infinitely indebted to you for another such offer."

The Yankees valued education so much so that they often presumed to more learning than they really had and exposed themselves as pretentious pseudo-intellectuals. Although the Yankees established common schools and enjoyed widespread literacy, in Cooper's view the education was superficial, substituting shallow learning for common sense and failing to produce the really educated men needed for leadership. They valued and craved respectability more than independence, as Solzhenitsyn would observe to be an American characteristic in the next century. Cooper has good fun relating how the Yankee newcomers changed "Satanstoe," a colorful name given by the earliest settlers, to the "respectable" Dibbleton. They could organize to get things done and bring about change, whether other people wanted it or not. (New Englanders still tout themselves as people who get together to change the world.)

One of Coopers characters, who has painfully observed the dubious methodology of Jason's rise to wealth and power, comments:

> I never could explain the process by means of which Jason wound his way into everybody's secrets. . . . The people of New England have a reputation this way . . . everything and everybody were brought under rigid church government among the Puritans; and when a whole community gets the notion that it is to sit in judgment on every act of one of its members, it is quite natural that it should extend that right into an enquiry into all his affairs. One thing is certain: our neighbours of Connecticut do assume a control over the acts and opinions of individuals that is not dreamed of in New York.

Thus Cooper identified the historical origins of the perpetual crusades for the reform and reconstruction of society that diminish American liberty and independence to this day.

There is a convention of American history writing that aristocracy in American politics was replaced by "democracy" when Andrew Jackson was elected president in 1828, bringing a wild new popular spirit to American government. For Cooper, and for many others, this was not the case at all. General Jackson was a natural aristocrat. Like Washington, he thought for himself and did not court the wealthy or public acclaim (which he already had), but he pursued a fearless, independent course. Jackson was a self-made aristocrat, a spectacularly successful patriotic warrior and master of a plantation.

Cooper perceived the rise of irresponsible democracy differently, and foresaw many of the defects that later became pervasive in the processes of American government. The fall from grace came not from Jacksonian Democrats but from the Whigs, devoted at the same time to money-making by any means and moralistic hectoring of other Americans. In 1840 those who had perverted politics in New York went national. The Whigs wanted a tariff and national bank, which was largely a matter of profit for certain interests. But, they dared not proclaim their real agenda. So they met, declined to adopt any platform, and nominated Gen. William Henry Harrison, a politically naive military hero whose successes had occurred a quarter century before. They conducted the election with meaningless uproar—torchlight parades with log cabins (in which they falsely claimed their hero had born) and jugs of cider (which their hero allegedly drank), with marching bands and a catchy, meaningless slogan, "Tippecanoe and Tyler Too." When the Whigs elected Harrison, as the result of a recession and the unpopularity of his opponent Martin Van Buren, their real leader Henry Clay proclaimed that the election results were a popular mandate for an increased tariff and a new national bank, which had been barely mentioned in the campaign.

American elections had thus become carnivals in which real issues were not addressed, and contests between candidates were carefully picked by party managers. In fact, politics was now completely in the hands of party managers representing selfish interests and claiming falsely to represent the will of the people. For Cooper, the rule of party machinery was not democracy. Rather, it subverted the Founders' intent that elections were to choose men of proven integrity, patriotism, and independence of mind. He wrote:

> Demagogues are a highly privileged class. The editors of newspapers are another privileged class; doing things, daily and hourly, which set all law and justice at defiance, and invading, with perfect impunity, the most precious rights of their fellow-citizens. The power of both is enormous, and, as in all cases of great and irresponsible power, both enormously abuse it. . . . In a democracy, misleading the publick mind, as regards, facts, characters, or principles is corrupting all that is dear to society at its source. . . . Discreet and observing men have questioned whether, after excluding the notices of deaths and marriages, one half of the circumstances that are related in the newspapers of America, as facts, are true in their essential features. . . . If newspapers are useful in overthrowing tyrants, it is only to establish a tyranny of their own.

Furthermore, it was a mistake to think that political parties are necessary to liberty. Parties churned up unnecessary strife and dragooned people into supporting positions they would not ordinarily take except for party discipline:

> It is a very different thing to be a democrat, and to be a member of what is called a democratic party. . . . The great body of the nation has no real interest in party. . . . No freeman, who really loves liberty and who has a just perception of its dignity, character, action, and objects, will ever become a mere party man.

This was the time when the witticism became popular that "The U.S. House of Representatives was no place for a gentleman." For Cooper and others who adhered to an older standard, this was a bitter truth.

It was the Whigs—the party of business—the people behind all the disagreeable developments that had confronted Cooper in New York, and not the Democrats—advocates of states' rights and laissez-faire—who had vulgarized and subverted American democracy. After Cooper's time, the Republicans succeeded the Whigs. In 1860, at the Republican National Convention in Chicago, candidate Abraham Lincoln, a spokesman for tariffs, national banks, and railroads, appeared on the platform with his step-brother, who displayed rails allegedly split by Lincoln as a young man. The "Rail-Splitter" was just an ordinary working guy that any Northern working guy could identify with, (though local people said that Lincoln had split fewer rails than any man in the county). And the prospective voters were lured by an open appeal to appetite: "Vote Yourself a Farm!" Such behavior was unthinkable for Washington, Jefferson, Jackson, Franklin Pierce, James Buchanan, or Jefferson Davis.

"A Yankee is never satisfied unless he is making changes," says one of Cooper's characters. "One half of his time, he is altering the pronunciation of his own names, and the other half he is altering ours." Like many others of the time, Cooper deplored the Noah Webster campaign to reduce American regional pronunciations and spellings to an artificial New England standard.

"I doubt if all this craving for change has not more of selfishness in it than either of expediency or philosophy," wrote Cooper, an insight that strikes a chord with conservatives of all times. The Connecticut newcomers, it seems, regarded themselves as more righteous than the sinful New Yorkers among whom they settled, and therefore felt that they were entitled to change their ways and appropriate their property. It was a normal means of proceeding in their Puritan heritage for the Yankees to justify themselves by portraying those who opposed them as bad people with evil motives. "These men inevitably quarrel with all above them, and, with them, to quarrel is to calumniate." The "Chainbearer," a venerable surveyor as honest and benevolent as the day is long, finds that he has become known as "an old rogue" among people who have never even met him— slander spread because of his opposition to Jason's schemes. Over his self-reverential agenda, the Yankee "throws a beautiful halo of morality and religion, never even prevaricating in the hottest discussion, unless with the unction of a saint."

The Yankee immigrants to New York State had in fact created the phenomenon of "the Burnt Over District," well-known to Americans at the time. Western New York was thus labeled because it had been swept over by so many furious fires of evangelism and reform. Such phenomena as Anti-Masonry, Mormonism, prohibition, vegetarianism, Seventh Day Adventism, socialism, and feminism all had their origins in the Burnt Over District. And finally abolitionism as the region became the base for John Brown's terrorism. Like most moderate Northerners, Cooper regarded agitation against slavery in the South as unconstitutional, unwise, and counter-productive. He agreed with John Adams that American slavery was mild and that slaves were no worse off than the lower class of Northern workers. He comments of slavery:

> It is an evil, certainly, but in a comparative sense, not as great an evil as is usually imagined. There is scarcely a nation of Europe that does not possess institutions that inflict as gross personal privations and wrongs, as the slavery of America. . . . It is quite possible to be an excellent Christian and a slaveholder.

When Cooper wrote in *The American Democrat* that "the union of these States is founded on an express compromise, and it is not its intention to reach a benefit, however considerable, by extorting undue sacrifices from particular members of the confederacy," he doubtless had in mind the Whig "protective" tariff that exploited the South. And Cooper assumed (as did Tocqueville and countless other non-Southerners) it to be uncontested that the Union was "a compact between separate communities"—something that was later claimed to be an artificial Southern position.

For Cooper, the greedy rent-seekers through government and

the moralistic reformers were but two sides of the same coin in the subverting of American liberty: "The American *doctrinaire* is the converse of the American demagogue, and, in his way, is scarcely less injurious to the publick. . . . These opposing classes produce the effect of all counter-acting forces, resistance, and they provoke each others' excesses." He was describing the sham battles between "liberals" and "conservatives" that make up most of American politics almost two centuries later. "Democracy" of this new sort had brought the politicization of social and moral life into campaigns for the alleged improvements that were necessary for "democracy" to be fulfilled. This was contrary to the individual liberty that Cooper believed the American founding had intended. It made "democracy" into a crusade rather than a legal framework of freedom—it was all about power rather than liberty.

"The end of liberty is the happiness of man," wrote James Fenimore Cooper, "and its means, that of leaving the greatest possible personal freedom of action, that comports with the general good." Americans have "democracy," he added, but they are more under the rule of extra-legal authority than almost any people in the world. The all-important question was "whether principles are to rule this republic, or men; and these last, too, viewed in their most vulgar and repulsive qualities. . . . It is time that the American began to see things as they are, not as they are said to be, in the speeches of governors, fourth of July orations, and electioneering addresses."

Condy Raguet: Apostle of Free Trade and Free Banking

The love of money is said to be the root of all evil. It is also nearly universal. Money is not the only cause of action in human affairs, but it is unwise to ignore it when seeking to understand history. "Money" is deeply involved in such weighty questions as how much credit is available in an economy and at what rate of interest; government spending, taxation, borrowing, and debt; conditions of trade (the facilitation of trade being the origin of money); the working of supply and demand and thus the prices that we all pay for goods and receive for our labor; and the related phenomenon of inflation/deflation.

Money is a measure of wealth. As a measure it is primarily a value, an intangible, else it could not be represented by a nearly worthless scrap of paper. Thus money is not so much a thing in itself as a concept in the minds of men. Men may disagree about concepts and how they are generally understood may change over time—in history.

Money winds through the life of the United States. The experience of "not worth a Continental," referring to the depreciated paper that in part financed the War of Independence, played an important role in persuading the states to establish the Constitution. Alexander Hamilton thought banks were necessary for national strength and prosperity, while Thomas Jefferson warned that bank-notes, the money issued by banks, would become as plentiful and as worthless as oak leaves. Andrew Jackson declared that real money was metallic and a "Monster Bank" was a threat to the public good, but William Jennings Bryan proclaimed that Americans must not "be crucified on a cross of gold." Regulation of the "money supply" was a contentious question through the twentieth century into our own time.

There are three serious obstacles to understanding the role of money in public affairs and in history. The first is the profession or academic discipline of "economists," a fairly recent historical development. Economists profess to represent a science that provides reliable knowledge. But, because they disagree among themselves and they are not notably successful in their predictions, we may doubt that.

The second obstacle has to do with the fact that in a large national economy there are countless variables, known and unknown and constantly changing. Thus sequences are not always consequences. That B follows A does not necessarily prove that A is the cause of B. However, that is what politicians customarily want us to believe: prosperity is a result of their programs and a lack of prosperity is the fault of their opponents. It is doubtful that the class of politicians in general either knows or cares what is actually the economic truth.

The third obstacle is the well-known phenomenon of "rent-seeking." There are always interests that seek to make money from government actions, but such interests invariably have benevolent-sounding reasons, prolifically publicized, to persuade that their raids on the public treasury are desirable for the general good. A classic example is Alexander Hamilton's statement that "a public debt is a public blessing."

Unfortunately, the role of money in American history has generally been told as a story of the charges and counter-charges of politicians. Condy Raguet, however, sought assiduously to understand economics as a matter of principle apart from all political advantage and to show the compatibility of free markets with republican liberty and equality and the American Constitution. Though nearly forgotten, he was an early and great American economist (of the genuine sort) and is very worthy of attention for his views of major issues of antebellum American politics: the tariff, government spending and debt, banking and currency, and economic regulation.

Condy Raguet was born in 1784 to an established Philadelphia family of French-Huguenot origin. After attending the University of Pennsylvania, he went to sea as a supercargo on merchant vessels before setting up his own mercantile business. One result of his voyaging was two pamphlets (1804, 1805) and several articles describing conditions in Santo Domingo after the black revolution there. Evidently, Raguet's expertise in trade and languages came to the attention of President Monroe, who in 1821 appointed him U.S. Consul at Rio de Janeiro. Subsequently Raguet was promoted to *chargè d'affaires*, or in effect the first U.S. Minister to Brazil.

In 1827, he returned to Philadelphia where he remained an active businessman, civic leader, journalist, and scholar until his death in 1842. He served in the legislature, for which he wrote an important report on banking. For a time he was president of the chamber of commerce and was elected a member of the prestigious American Philosophical Society. Most notably, Raguet established and served as president of the first savings bank in the United States, the Philadelphia Savings Fund Society, a successful alternative to commercial banks that was widely copied.

Raguet's study of economics was prompted by the Panic of 1819, which lasted for five years. Banks closed, businesses failed, trade stagnated, property values and agricultural prices were cut in half, and unemployment reached critical proportions in the cities. The experience of this devastating depression underlay American thinking about economics for the next several decades, although not everyone drew the same conclusions as to causes—a situation that continues to this day.

Philadelphia in the antebellum period was the center of both free market and protectionist thinking and journalism. On the protection side was the formidable father and son publishing team of Matthew and Henry Carey. Matthew Carey (1760-1839) was the major American proponent of a large, aggressive navy to spread and protect American power and trade around the world. He made little headway against Jeffersonians, who saw a navy as expensive, potentially dangerous, and unnecessary, because its only mission should be to defend the coasts and not to force American manufactured products on reluctant foreigners.

Henry C. Carey (1793-1879) was more successful as a prolific and plausible advocate of "tariff protection." He believed that a strong economy could and should be built by subsidizing business directly as well as indirectly with a tariff (tax on imports) that made foreign goods so expensive that all Americans would be forced to buy domestic manufactured products. Carey was the leading publicist for the "American System," a political platform that played a large role in American affairs in the years prior to the War Between the States. The American System called for a "national bank," a high protective tariff to support domestic manufactures, and subsidies of business for building infrastructure ("internal improvements"). An energetic government, not too bothered by Constitutional limitations, thus would supposedly bring into being a powerful, self-reliant America.

The program was presented as a question of patriotism and it was claimed that it would guarantee high wages for labor and high prices for farmers' produce as well as prosperity for business. Some Congressional representatives of New England manufacturers even declared that to oppose the tariff identified one as a traitor. (Henry Carey was later to argue, oddly, that free trade had caused the Civil War. If only the United States had had a higher and more consistent tariff, the South would have been forced to become more like the North and there would have been no war.)

Condy Raguet was among the most active and eloquent opponents of every aspect of the "American System." Such a policy, using the government to force the economy and society into a pattern predetermined by self-appointed wise and patriotic men, whether capitalist or socialist, was exactly what Raguet and other free traders objected to. It was a threat to both prosperity and liberty. The claims of patriotism and universal benefit for the system ignored that it gave special privilege and profit to certain economic activities at the expense of others—especially those of the South, which provided nearly all of the Union's foreign trade by its exports, and the related Northern merchants. The claims flouted the free market dictum that government subsidies distort markets rather than bringing general prosperity.

Raguet and a group of Philadelphia scholars, including his brilliant friend William M. Gouge, who also should be better known, became a dynamic center of free economy thinking in the United States, rivaled only perhaps by South Carolina writers. Another member of the Philadelphia free trade company was Charles J. Ingersoll, who long served in the U.S. House of Representatives where he was chairman of the Committee on Foreign Relations. These collegial scholars absorbed and applied to American conditions and discourse the cutting-edge wisdom of Adam Smith, David Ricardo, Jean-Baptiste Say, and other European thinkers. Raguet published two important pioneer treatises in American economic thought: *The Principles of Free Trade* (1835) and *On Currency and Banking* (1839). He also published a series of journals from 1829 through the 1830s: *The Banner of the Constitution, The Free Trade Advocate,* and *The Examiner and Journal of Political Economy*. Raguet was an insightful, hard-hitting commentator on current economic assertions and political maneuverings, often resorting to lively and telling satire.

A major issue between the two schools was the status of

corporations. Corporations were artificial persons that had great legal rights but very limited liability. Traditionally, corporations had been centers of privilege and abuse of the broader public. The Constitutional Convention of 1787 considered but voted down giving the proposed federal government the delegated power to charter corporations. This did not prevent Alexander Hamilton and his friends from chartering "a Bank of the United States" as "necessary and proper" for carrying out delegated powers. This was the first issue that galvanized a Jeffersonian opposition, which eventually led to the expulsion of the Federalists from power. As John Taylor of Caroline pointed out, Hamilton had assumed that the federal government was sovereign by "means" even though it was forbidden sovereignty as to "ends."

Once established, corporations became largely untouchable, especially because the Federalists had worked into the Constitution a federal guarantee of "the sanctity of contracts." However, the same capitalist interests who relied on the "sanctity of contracts" to protect them from government regulation also pushed relentlessly for bankruptcy laws that would relieve them of the consequences of bad contracts.

Legislators "positively fancy that human laws are omnipotent, that anything and everything can be accomplished by the vote of a majority," wrote Raguet. No law or act of government could possibly create real prosperity, which was the work of human labor and intelligence. The preference of Raguet and his colleagues for government non-interference in the economy was not merely a conviction of correct theory. They were not simply enamored of a doctrine of maximum utility. Their view was ethical, republican, and Constitutional. Every aspect of the American System was wrong. It could only transfer wealth from one group to another, violating liberty and the legal equality necessary for a free society. They were expressing what they saw as the true American principles.

Raguet believed that conferring special privileges upon corporations laid "the foundation of an *artificial* inequality of wealth, and thereby, of *artificial* inequality of power." William Gouge avowed that "the moment that two or more individuals are associated by act of law and endowed with privileges which do not belong to them as individuals, all natural, social, and political equality is destroyed for their advantage and to the prejudice to the rest of the community." Raguet put it thus in regard to banking corporations:

the moral sense of corporations cannot be relied upon for the protection of the public. The ignorance of some, the speculative arrogance of others, the favouritism incident to most, and the desire common to all, to amass large profits, are constantly operating to effect an expansion of the currency to the utmost limits of tension: and however prudently and wisely conducted may be many of these institutions, their influence is lost upon the rest, and when a calamity befalls the country by a general stoppage of payments, they are made to share in the common catastrophe.

Federal "internal improvements" expenditures for roads and canals had been deemed unconstitutional by every great man of the Jeffersonian party, and President Madison had reiterated that point in one of his last official acts. But some states had invested heavily in such projects, and some expenditures on a small scale occasionally made their way through Congress. For the free-market men, such government projects merely enriched some people and distorted the natural course of investment. They had a point—several states scandalously defaulted on their debts after committing to canal projects that were rendered useless by the development of railroads.

Raguet's position on the national bank controversy of Andrew Jackson's administration sheds a very informative light upon the differences between economic knowledge and partisan commentary on complex matters, whether by politicians or historians. Few people at the time or later understood the laws of currency better than Raguet. The "national bank" was not a government bank, but a government-chartered private organization (like the Federal Reserve of later times). The government chose the president and one-fifth of the board of directors in exchange for providing one-fifth of the capital. Most importantly, the bank had the very profitable privilege of doing the government's banking business, *i.e.,* of holding the government's money on deposit. This gave its bank-notes great soundness.

The creation of a corporation in the states, before general incorporation laws, required a special act of the legislature. Some states began to charter corporations freely, especially banks, notably in Pennsylvania. This created the phenomenon of "fractional-reserve banking." Assuming that not all depositors would call for their money at the same time, banks could loan out at interest far more funds than they actually had. They were in effect expanding the money supply by creating credit in the form of paper money promising a largely imaginary redeemability in hard money. The effect was inevitably inflationary. The issuing bankers profited greatly, but the last holders of the notes might find themselves with worthless paper. The bankers could suspend payments and go into irresponsible bankruptcy with their profits. Most people thought of banks as places where money was deposited and lent out again, not realizing that they had become money machines. In the discussions of the time, "state banks" generally refered not to government organizations but to private institutions with state charters. Historians have often missed this point. It becomes even more interesting when one notes that the states are forbidden by the Constitution to issue "bills of credit," but they were chartering private and semi-private corporations that were in effect exercising that privilege.

It was believed by many Americans, at least until the chickens came home to roost, that expansive bank credit was a desirable thing, even a necessary thing to develop the economy. In his *A Treatise on Currency and Banking*, which was a result of study of the panic in Pennsylvania that was presented to the legislature, Raguet argued that this was a fallacy—that such inflation merely created a boom-and-bust cycle and profited bankers without contributing to solid economic growth. The boom had been created by unnatural credit expansion, resulting inevitably in the Panic of 1819. He surveyed every county and found that the public agreed. A majority believed that the banks were more harmful than beneficial. Raguet argued vigorously that future bank charters should contain strong restrictions on fractional reserve banking. Even better, the banking business, like every other business, should be open to anyone— "free banking" without the need for legal incorporation. When such free banks misbehaved they would quickly be disciplined by the market. In the long-run Raguet failed to make much impact. The U.S. economy developed into a permanent boom-and-bust phenomenon in which private banking interests enjoy enormous power and profit.

The British economist David Ricardo read Raguet's works and wrote to him. Ricardo was puzzled. How could American banks get away with churning out unsupported paper? Why did not someone present the notes to the bank and demand that they be redeemed in real money at face value? It was simple, Raguet replied. Nearly all the well-to-do and influential people in the community were complicit in the bank as stockholders, depositors, and borrowers. A threat to the bank was a threat to the community and would bring vicious economic and social retaliation.

The second national bank (1816-36), like the later Federal Reserve, was unconstitutional and a grant of too much power and guaranteed profit to private interests. However, most of the time, it was under able administration and served useful purposes. Its notes were at par. They fulfilled (indirectly) Congress's duty to provide a sound circulating medium and facilitated trade by obviating the need for inconvenient shipments of gold and silver. Further, the bank provided a useful check on excessive paper issues of the "state banks" by grading their decline from face value. This curbing of their activities was resented by New York bankers who had the ear of Vice Pres. Martin Van Buren.

Many people held the national bank responsible for the Panic of 1819, including Pres. Andrew Jackson, who had suffered badly in the crisis. This belief was dubious, but Jackson's belief that the bank's president Nicholas Biddle had exerted political influence against Jackson was better founded (though Biddle's actions were defensive only). The charter of the bank was subject to renewal by Congress in 1836. Henry Clay, leader of the "American System," got through Congress a re-charter act several years in advance, a measure that was not unreasonable but was clearly politically motivated. Jackson supposedly declared that the bank was trying to kill him but that he would kill it instead. Out of the blue, he denounced the bank as evil, vetoed the re-charter, and then went further. He removed all the government's deposits of money from the national bank, where they rested by law. William J. Duane, a member of the Philadelphia free market circle and Jackson's Secretary of the Treasury, refused to carry out Jackson's unlawful order and resigned. Jackson went through a number of appointees before he found a Secretary of the Treasury who would comply.

Jackson's action is still praised as a blow in favor of sound money based on gold and silver. He may have thought so, but it was anything but. The country was faced with the question of what to do with the government's money, a perpetual source of conflict and a target of potential profit for designing men. Jackson's solution was to place the government's banking business in a collection of state banks chosen by his administration. This lacked the sanction of law and was viewed as a dangerous exercise of executive patronage. The

Senate censured the president for his arbitrary and illegal actions.

Even worse, the favored banks with their windfall of funds expanded credit freely, bringing on the inevitable bust in the Panic of 1836. Raguet and his school of free bankers understood and elucidated all this clearly, but they had limited influence on the ensuing political conflicts because they condemned both the Whig national bankers and the Democrat state bankers. Raguet wrote that Jackson "affects to dread a monied aristocracy; he complained of the corruption of one bank, and yet takes forty or fifty irresponsible paper-circulating banks under the national wing." Duane said that the bank matter was not initiated by the president, who did not understand what he was doing, but was designed by selfish men around him. The rhetoric was about "hard money" but the political push reflected the input of New York and other state bankers who resented the national bank's power. Raguet and friends were better "Jacksonian Democrats" in opposition to special privilege than were Jackson and others who have been praised by historians as heroes of democracy.

Nowhere was Raguet more incisive and eloquent than in his case against "tariff protection." The placing of high taxes on imports so that consumers would be compelled to buy American-made products was a perversion of the Constitution. Congress had been given the power to collect import duties for the support of the government, not to give special favors to certain interests. Why should people be required by law to pay more for the goods they purchased in order "to make a few men richer? Can this be government of the people. . . . Is it not rather a burlesque upon the right of self-government?" By what magic formula did "manufactures" somehow deserve special government favors when the rest of the "industries" carried on by the vast majority of Americans did not? The tariff hurt everyone, including the general Northern public, although most failed to understand that, under the barrage of patriotic prosperity propaganda.

Of course, exposing the fallacy of tariff protection did not eliminate it as a political program. People are always able to provide benevolent-sounding reasons to justify government policies from which they profit. Demands for the protective tariff appeared after the War of 1812 and rose steadily, with organized lobbies of manufacturing interests infesting the lobbies of Congress. Raguet was vivid in describing the "lobbyists" for New England textile manufacturers and Pennsylvania iron men as conniving enemies of the public good.

Demand for "tariff protection" resulted finally in the 1828 "Tariff of Abominations," as egregious an act of log-rolling, exploitation, special interests, and political chicanery as is possible to imagine. The law was widely protested, though most opposition was not willing to go as far as South Carolina did in its protest. That state immediately began a process leading to the nullification of this law, and in 1832 did just that. Raguet and his Philadelphia free-market circle were among the small number of Northerners who vigorously and publically supported South Carolina through the crisis.

The adverse effects of the tariff had even worse consequences than enrichment of the few at the expense of the many. In the American situation the benefits and burdens of the protective tariff were regionalized. Powerful elements in the Northeast profited and the South paid, which was an obvious threat to the comity of the Union. Raguet and friends were seriously concerned with the inequity as a cause of sectional discord. Southerners were less selfish patriots and better economists than the manufacturers and their political servants, of whom he wrote:

> Instead of listening to the appeals of their fellow citizens of the South, who feel themselves aggrieved . . . as common justice and patriotic sympathy demand they should do, they turn a deaf and indifferent ear, and relying on their numerical power to outvote the complainants, they virtually adopt the principle that the constitution is precisely that which a majority of the Congress shall pronounce it to be.

The protectionists and other rising powers of the Northern economy cared nothing for the comity of the Union. Southerners were not fellow citizens with a right to a say, but merely raw material for national greatness and obstacles to be removed. In 1834, Matthew Carey threatened the Southern people with fire and sword if they did not accept continued increases in the tariff. The historian H. A. Scott Trask has written:

> Carey had reminded them [Southerners] that Northerners were superior in numbers and in warships and could easily subdue them with superior military force if necessary; in particular Carey had pointed out how easy it would be for Northern troops to penetrate the long exposed Southern coastline. He [Raguet] quoted one of Carey's more memorable questions: "What is to defend your exposed coast from hostile irruptions and desolation?"

Enraptured by the economic and emotional force of nationalism, it did not occur to Carey that the Constitution had established a limited government and a union that was supposed to be of benefit to all regions. Carey's policy would be precisely and fully implemented by Lincoln later (although not as easily as imagined), which casts an interesting light on the popular theory that the War Between the States was all about slavery and nothing but slavery.

Raguet had passed from the scene but his associates continued through the antebellum conflicts and the war to boldly and eloquently oppose Republican policies and the war on the South, which they saw as not preserving the Union but destroying it. They maintained their position in the face of Republican ballot-stuffing and mob violence, and they gathered a considerable following as the war went badly and Republican promises seemed more and more false.

One of Raguet's disciples, Edward Ingersoll, on the day before Lincoln's assassination, gave a speech in which he denounced the war and defended the right of secession as a legacy of the Founding Fathers. The Republican press howled that Ingersoll was in league with John Wilkes Booth. A few weeks later, Ingersoll was assaulted by a mob on a Philadelphia street and severely beaten. The police stood by until the beating was over and then took Ingersoll to jail for assault and battery. When two lawyers came to see him, they too were attacked by a mob, as was his brother Charles. The Republican president of the city council remarked that it was "not the business of loyal men to go out of their way to save disloyal men from the consequences of their conduct."

The American System had some legislative successes during the antebellum period but was usually held back by lingering Jeffersonian beliefs. It was not fully established until the 1860s, when Lincoln and the Republicans could legislate without Southern opposition. They at once implemented a high tariff, a "national banking" system, and munificent subsidies for politically connected capitalists. Even so, Condy Raguet had made a case against state capitalism and for economic freedom that still rings true.

True American Whiggery: John Tyler and Abel P. Upshur

Two dates changed the course of American political history. On 13 September 1841, the Whigs expelled Pres. John Tyler from their party, outraged over his "betrayal" of what they considered true Whig political and economic principles. Shorty more than two years later, on 28 February 1844, Abel P. Upshur, Tyler's trusted Secretary of State and perhaps the best Constitutional scholar in the United States at the time, was killed in an accident on the U.S.S. *Princeton*. Both men personified American Whiggery and both are forgotten or maligned by the modern American historical profession. Historians generally consider Tyler's presidency to be an abject failure while Upshur receives mention only in regard to his tragic death and his defense of slavery. Philosophically, however, their brand of States' Rights Whiggery helped form the backbone of the American political tradition.

The Whig Party was initially a loose coalition of forces united by their opposition to Andrew Jackson. Historians give credit to New York newspaperman James Watson Webb for coming up with the name in 1834, but in reality "Whig" was used two years before that in South Carolina by advocates of nullification. The term, of course, implied that those who supported "King Andrew" and a powerful executive branch were "Tories." This had a profound rhetorical effect as most Americans identified the term "Tory" with the British side of the American War for Independence. That was the point. Unfortunately, the men who later dominated the Whig Party and who kicked Tyler out in 1841, namely the former National Republicans led by Henry Clay, John Quincy Adams, and Daniel Webster, supported the same type of system they publically railed against. They hijacked the name. Historians have for decades classified the Whig Party as the conservative antithesis to "Jacksonian democracy," and this classification was accurate in 1841 when Tyler assumed office after the death of William Henry Harrison. That Whig Party died when Tyler left office in 1845.

John Tyler, Jr., was reared in the American political tradition. Born on 29 March 1790 at his family plantation in Charles City County, Virginia, he was descended from a prominent Virginia family. His father, John Tyler, Sr., roomed with Thomas Jefferson at the College of William and Mary, was an anti-Constitution delegate to the Virginia Ratifying Convention of 1788, served in the Virginia House of Delegates and as Governor of Virginia, and later was appointed by James Madison to the federal court system. He was a well-known Jeffersonian and advocate of a limited central government.

Tyler, Jr., followed his father to the College of William and Mary where he was graduated at age seventeen and was admitted to the Virginia bar in 1809 at age nineteen. He was elected to the Virginia House of Delegates at age twenty-one and later to the United States House of Representatives in 1816 where he served three consecutive terms. He was appointed Governor of Virginia in 1825 and United States Senator from Virginia in 1827, where he served until 1836. After a brief retirement from public life, Tyler was nominated by the Whig Party for Vice President of the United States in 1840. He was placed on the ticket in order to persuade Southern States' Rights advocates to vote for the Whig Party in the election. It worked. The Whigs won the election in 1840 with Tyler later assuming office after the death of William Henry Harrison in 1841.

Critics called him "His Accidency," and were frustrated with Tyler's intractability on core "Whig" programs such as a national bank, federally funded internal improvements, and high tariffs. They should have expected no less. His political career was a testament to decentralization and states' rights, what he called the "principle" of "our Revolution," and opposition to the Hamiltonian system. While in the Virginia House of Delegates in 1811, Tyler backed the censure of Virginia's two senators, Richard Brent and William Giles, because they voted to re-charter the Bank of the United States in complete disregard to their instructions from the state legislature. Tyler considered the bank unconstitutional and insisted that by their action, Brent and Giles had ceased "to be the true and legitimate representatives of this State."

Tyler consistently voted against nationalist legislation while serving in the United States House of Representatives. He opposed federally funded internal improvements—"Virginia," he said, was not "in so poor a condition as to require a *charitable* donation from Congress"—fought against increases in Congressional salaries, argued that any surplus in the treasury should be used to reduce taxes and to pay off the national debt, and served on a committee charged with auditing the Second Bank of the United States. Tyler concluded after the audit that the Bank charter was "most shamefully perverted to the purposes of stock-jobbing and speculation." His position was consistent with his Jeffersonian principles, and in a lengthy speech on the issue he declared that the Bank was "a system not to be supported by any correct principles of political economy . . . [and has] more to corrupt the morals of society than anything else." Corruption of the principles of the Revolution was the key to his argument. "Our Republic can only be preserved by a strict adherence to virtue. It is our duty . . . to put down the first instance of detected corruption, and thereby to preserve ourselves from its contamination." As for the debt, Tyler hoped that "The day . . . has passed, in which a national debt was esteemed a national blessing."

By the time Tyler was appointed to the United States Senate, he was already regarded as a principled Jeffersonian, and he did nothing to damage his reputation as a United States Senator from Virginia. He continued to fight against federally funded internal improvements and crystallized his definition of Union. He considered the United States a republic of sovereign states and criticized those who regarded the United States as a singular nation. "I have no such word [national] in my political vocabulary," he said in May 1830. "A nation of twenty-four nations is an idea which I cannot realize. A confederacy may embrace many nations; but by what process twenty-four can be converted into one, I am still to learn."

But his greatest fight for the principles of Jeffersonianism was yet to come. As early as 1820, Tyler warned of the evils of protectionism. Protective tariffs, he argued, only enriched industrialists while impoverishing the agricultural class. The wisest course was to pursue a policy where foreign markets were encouraged to purchase both American agricultural and manufactured goods, thus boosting consuming power in the United States. This could only be accomplished through low, revenue-only tariffs. His arguments and those of the other Jeffersonians fell on deaf ears. The 1828 tariff, called the "Tariff of Abominations" by South Carolina, and the 1832 tariff were the highest to that point in American history. Tyler opposed both, insisting that the end result would be the destruction of the agricultural interests of the United States. This, he said, would only antagonize the sections of the United States and would do little to produce the economic bounty the protectionists promised.

At the heart of each blow Tyler delivered to the Hamiltonian system was the insistence that Hamiltonianism, be it protective tariffs, federally funded internal improvements, or central banking, was nothing more than useless reform that perverted the ideals of the American federal republic and the principles of 1776. Historians have often tried to paint Jeffersonian political-economy as reactionary, and in particular a veiled defense of slavery, but Tyler never described it in those terms, nor did most Jeffersonians. He favored agriculture and the independence of the American people, neither of which could be maintained by high taxes, "stock jobbers," or centralization. This was American conservatism, pure and simple, and while it was best expressed by Southerners, it was by no means sectional.

Tyler's break with the Democrats occurred during the nullification "crisis" of 1832-33. He had always displayed an independent streak and had been a resolute opponent of unconstitutional executive action. Andrew Jackson's response to nullification shook his faith in the Constitution and the Union. Tyler did not support nullification (he preferred secession), but when Jackson called for the use of force to collect the tariff, Tyler could not stand idly by and watch a sister state placed under the federal heel. He wrote in 1833:

> If South Carolina be put down then may each of the States yield all pretentions to sovereignty. We have a consolidated government, and a master will soon arise. This is inevitable. How idle to talk of preserving a republic for any length of time with an uncontrolled power over the military, exercised at pleasure by the President.

He cast the lone vote against the Force Bill in the Senate and made the only speech in opposition. Friends warned him against such a course, but Tyler's sense of obligation to the Union of the Founders and his fear of a "consolidated military despotism" drove his actions in 1833.

In his long speech against the Force Bill, Tyler outlined his understanding of the Constitution. "The government was created by the States, is amenable by the States, is preserved by the States, and may be destroyed by the States.... They may strike [the Federal government] out of existence by a word; demolish the Constitution and scatter its fragments to the winds." He called on the examples of the American War for Independence and implored Congress heed those lessons:

> It is an argument of pride to say that the government should not yield while South Carolina is showing a spirit of revolt. It was just such an argument that was used against the American colonies by the British government—an argument spoken against by Burke and Pitt. . . . But it is a bad mode of settling disputes to make soldiers your ambassadors, and to point to the halter and the gallows as your ultimatum.

Tyler's reference to Burke and Pitt is important. Both men were loosely affiliated with the Whig faction in British politics, or those who opposed absolute monarchy, and both men, principally Burke, are regarded as intellectual heirs of modern conservatism, what Russell Kirk famously labeled the "Conservative Mind" in 1953. This "Conservative Mind" was best expressed by what would become the states' rights faction of the American Whig Party. Tyler classified his political ideology as Jeffersonianism. As he said in 1860, "I belonged, in short, to the old Jeffersonian party, from whose principles of constitutional construction I have never, in one single instance, departed." This conservative adherence to the principles of 1776 determined his course as President of the United States.

In good Jeffersonian form, Tyler was at his plantation when informed of the death of William Henry Harrison in April 1841. He hoped that the Vice Presidency, a position regarded as little more than a ceremonial referee in the Senate, would give him a reprieve from politics. This was not to be the case. He immediately left for Washington and began preparations for his administration. His Whig counterparts in the cabinet thought Tyler should simply act as a rubber stamp for their nationalist economic program, but they should have understood Tyler's ideological disposition. He had a clear track record.

After Tyler twice vetoed bills incorporating a third Bank of the United States, the entire cabinet—with the exception of Daniel Webster—resigned, a move orchestrated by Henry Clay, and then expelled him from the party. Tyler also vetoed an internal improvements bill, vetoed a protective tariff bill, and nominated several states' rights Whigs to cabinet positions after the nationalists jumped ship. In this way, Tyler placed a Jeffersonian stamp on the executive office. If the Whigs had been true to their name, Tyler's actions would have been accepted without question. Clearly, the constitutionality of the Bank of the United States, a protective tariff, and federally funded internal improvements had been dubious at best. By vetoing this legislation, Tyler was following the parameters set forth by George Washington, *i.e.,* veto legislation that is unconstitutional and let everything else pass. He was not abusing executive authority and, as a man without a party, he could not be considered acting in a partisan spirit. He was simply being a consistent Jeffersonian. The nationalists couldn't stand it.

If Tyler was the political brawn in the states' rights faction of the Whig Party, then his Secretary of Navy and later Secretary of State Abel P. Upshur had the sharpest legal mind of the group. Upshur was born in 1791 in Northampton County, Va. His father served in the War of 1812 and in the Virginia legislature as a Federalist. Upshur attended the College of New Jersey until his expulsion in 1807 for participating in a student rebellion against the faculty. He later enrolled at Yale but was never graduated. He studied law under William Wirt and served in the Virginia House of Delegates from 1812-13 and again from 1825-27. Along with Tyler, Upshur participated in the Virginia Constitutional Convention of 1829-30 and voted against plans to make the document more democratic. From 1826-41, Upshur served on the Virginia supreme court. Like Tyler, Upshur consistently favored states' rights and decentralization and was chosen for a cabinet position precisely because of his close ideological connections with the president.

The "loose interpretation" of the Constitution made famous by Alexander Hamilton found its way into the American common law through John Marshall and Joseph Story, a Marshall protégé, and was later championed by Henry Clay, Daniel Webster, and Abraham Lincoln, all nationalist Whigs. Story, in 1833, published a seminal three-volume work on the Constitution, entitled *Commentaries on the Constitution of the United States.* Story became both famous and wealthy from this publication, and it was considered by many to be the standard interpretation of the Constitution. The Jeffersonians, however, thought it was nothing more than a thinly veiled codification of the nationalist interpretation of the document. Upshur took Story to task in 1840 and offered a counterweight to the nationalist vision of America, one that was truly Whiggish.

Upshur's short treatise on the Constitution, titled *A Brief*

Enquiry into the True Nature and Character of our Federal Government, did not receive the same notoriety as Story's, nor did Upshur believe it would. He wrote in the preface that he had little hope anyone would read his work or offer a "favorable reception, except from the very few who still cherish the principles which I have endeavored to re-establish." Upshur claimed no originality, but because Story's work had become so entrenched in American political-ideology, Upshur was original by offering an opinion that deviated from the nationalist fervor that swept the United States in 1840. He based his conclusions on "the authentic information from history, and from a train of reasoning, which will occur to every mind, on the facts which history discloses." Rather than a technical legal "commentary," Upshur's work was more accurately a narrative of American constitutionalism from the American War for Independence forward. It was a work of history aimed at re-establishing the proper place of the states in American politics and most importantly rekindling the spirit and principles of 1776.

Upshur's first order of business in his work was debunking the myth that Americans were "one people." This formed the basis of the nationalist argument. If Americans were "one people," then any piece of nationalist legislation, be it tariffs or federally funded internal improvements, could be justified on the grounds that it was best for the "nation" as a whole. Upshur contended that an American "nation" did not exist, and that by reading the preamble to the Constitution in such a way as to assume that the American "people" formed the government distorted the original federal republic. Upshur contends that Story's "desire to make 'the people of the United States' into one consolidated nation is so strong and predominant, that it breaks forth, often uncalled for, in every part of his work." It was often subtle, but without Story's work, the nationalist version of American history may not have gained much traction in the late antebellum period.

Upshur wrote that

> The *unity* contended for by the author no where appears, but is distinctly disaffirmed in every sentence. . . . The people of the American colonies were, in no conceivable sense, "one people. . . ." The colonies had no common legislature, no common treasury, no common military power, no common judiciatory. . . . Although they were all, alike, dependencies of the British crown, yet, even in the action of the parent country, in regard to them, they were recognized as separate and distinct.

All efforts in the colonial period to form a "general superintending government over them all" failed and each colony "was sovereign within its own territory; and to sum up all, in a single sentence, they had no direct political connexion with each other!"

Nationalists, Upshur writes, would counter that while this may have been true in the colonial period, by the time of the American War for Independence, the "American people" rallied around a Union and formed a "national" government in 1774, if not legally but in fact. Upshur considered this to be imaginative construction.

> Congress did not claim any legislative power whatever, nor could it have done so, consistently with the political relations which the colonies still acknowledged and desired to preserve. Its acts were in the form of *resolutions* and not in the form of *laws*; It *recommended* to its constituents whatever it believed to be for their advantage, but it *commanded* nothing. Each colony, and the people thereof, were at perfect liberty to act upon such recommendations or not, as they might think proper.

Upshur and the other Jeffersonians understood that the "imaginative construction" of the nationalists was ultimately designed to reduce the power of the states, long a hedge against the evils of centralization. Upshur argues that the people of the states during the American War for Independence "never lost sight of the fact that they were citizens of separate colonies, and never, even impliedly, surrendered that character, or acknowledged a different allegiance." Upshur was attempting to move the argument in a direction that favored decentralization. He did so by pointing out that even the Declaration of Independence, long considered by the nationalists as an action of the American "nation," was in fact a:

> more public, though not a more solemn affirmation of what she [Virginia] had previously done [on 12 June 1776]; a pledge to the whole world that what she had resolved on in her separate charter, she would unite with the other colonies in performing. She could not declare herself free and independent more directly, in that form, than she had already done, by asserting her sovereign and irresponsible power, in throwing off her former government, and establishing a new one for herself.

This held true for the other states as well.

And this was just the tip of the spear. Upshur expertly shredded Story's interpretation of the preamble to the Constitution by pointing out that the original wording explicitly recognized the states and while it was later shortened to "We the People" late in the Philadelphia Convention of 1787, that did not alter its meaning. Moreover, the delegates to the convention were appointed by the states so there was no question the Constitution was the work of the states, not the American people as a whole. It was ratified by the people of the states in convention and the states had a primary role in the document. "The Constitution is federative, in the power which framed it; federative in the power which adopted and ratified it; federative in the power which sustains and keeps it alive; federative in the power by which alone it can be altered or amended; and federative in the structure of all its departments." He then asks "In what respect . . . can it be justly called a consolidated or national government?" Again, Upshur contends only through imaginative construction.

Upshur reserved his best arguments in support of state sovereignty. The question of sovereignty was paramount in antebellum America. Madison attempted to appease opponents of the Constitution in 1788 by coming up with the idea of dual sovereignty (the central government was supreme in its sphere and the states in theirs), but nationalists such as Story knew the score and rejected this idea. If they could reduce the power of the states, they would have unlimited control of federal resources and a monopoly on power. While Upshur believed nationalists were "dazzled" by this possibility, he saw only danger in a supreme central authority without limits. "Shall the agent be permitted to judge of the extent of his own powers, without reference to his constituent?" Because the general government was created by the states, the states alone had the right to act as a final arbiter in any dispute. Both nullification and secession served as a final check on federal power, but neither destroyed the Constitution as many nationalists suggested. In fact, Upshur defended nullification as a way to "*prevent the Constitution from being violated by the general government*," in other words as a way to *save* the Constitution and the Union. Secession would have the same effect. "The act of secession does not break up the Constitution, except as to the seceding state." To Upshur, nullification and secession were in essence a conservative response to ambitious and illegal reform.

> As that Constitution was formed by sovereign states, they alone are authorized, whenever the question arises between them and their common government, to determine, in the last resort, what powers they intended to confer on it. This is an inseparable incident of

> sovereignty; a right which belongs to the states, simply because they have never surrendered it to any other power. But to render this right available for any good purpose, it is indispensably necessary to maintain the states in their proper position. If their people suffer them to sink into the insignificance of mere municipal corporations, it will be vain to invoke their protection against the gigantic power of the federal government. This is the point to which the vigilance of the people should be chiefly directed. Their highest interest is at home; their palladium is their own state governments. They ought to know that they can look nowhere else with perfect assurance of safety and protection. Let them then maintain those governments, not only in their rights, but in their dignity and influence.

Ultimately, Upshur contended that the Constitution, as interpreted by Story and other nationalists, would ruin liberty in America and would produce nothing more than monarchy. "If [Story's] principles be correct, if ours be, indeed, and consolidated and not a federative system, I, at least, have no praises to bestow on it. Monarchy in form, open and acknowledged, is infinitely preferable to monarchy in disguise." Fearfully, this monarchy would be controlled by the masses, by a tyranny of the majority that could oppress the minority population. Upshur considered majority rule acceptable at the state level, for states were generally homogenous. "But in a country so extensive as the United States, with great differences of character, interests, and pursuits, and with these differences, too, marked by geographical lines, a fair opportunity is afforded for the exercise of an oppressive tyranny, by the majority over the minority."

Upshur prophetically saw the course of government in the United States. He surmised that the legislature, aware that it had self-imposed restraint, would soon destroy those restraints. Yet, the legislature would not long retain them.

> In every age of the world, the few have found means to steal power from the many. But in *our* government, if it be indeed a consolidated one, such a result is absolutely inevitable. The powers which are expressly lodged in the executive, and the still greater powers which are assumed, because the Constitution does not expressly deny them, a patronage which has no limit, and acknowledges no responsibility, all these are quite enough to bring the legislature to the feet of the executive. Every new power, therefore, which is assumed by the *federal government,* does but add so much to the powers of the president. One

by one, the powers of the other departments are swept away, or are wielded only at the will of the executive. This is not speculation; it is history; and those who have been so eager to increase the powers, and to diminish the responsibilities, of the federal government, may know, from their own experience, that they have labored only to aggrandize the executive department, and raise the president above the people. That officer is not, by the Constitution, and never was designed to be, any thing more than a simple executive of the laws; but the principle which consolidates all power in the federal government clothes him with royal authority, and subjects every right and every interest of the people to his will. The boasted *balance,* which is supposed to be found in the separation and independence of the departments, is proved, even by our own experience, apart from all reasoning, to afford no sufficient security against this accumulation of powers. It is to be feared that the reliance which we place on it may serve to quiet our apprehensions, and render us less vigilant, than we ought to be, of the progress, sly, yet sure, which a vicious and cunning president may make towards absolute power.

This is why Upshur, Tyler, and other states' rights advocates joined the Whig Party. They could see in Andrew Jackson the natural course of political power taking place in the United States. They were the pure expression of Whiggery. Once this faction was rendered powerless, the nationalist Whigs destroyed American Whiggery, for in the presidency of Abraham Lincoln, a partisan Whig for much of his political career, Upshur's prophesies came to fruition. In this regard, the progressives of the twentieth century were correct that nationalism equaled reform. The Jeffersonian Whigs understood that and attempted to find a way to defeat it. The Democratic Party and the Whig Party, while appearing to be ideologically different, were, in fact, both the same nationalist party with differences only in the degree to which they supported centralization. States' rights Jeffersonian Whiggery was an attempt to make a final stand against consolidation. They lost and by losing sealed the fate of the United States.

"A Senator of Rome When Rome Survived:"
The Unknown Calhoun

Of the Great Triumvirate who dominated American public discourse from the War of 1812 till the mid-nineteenth century, John C. Calhoun was the first to depart the scene, in 1850. Henry Clay and Daniel Webster lived a few more years. In a generous eulogy for the man who had been his opponent for forty years, Webster, realizing that an epoch of American history was drawing to a close, called Calhoun "a Senator of Rome when Rome survived." Calhoun's aspirations were always "high, honorable, and noble," Webster said, and "nothing low or selfish" ever "came near the heart or the head of Mr. Calhoun."

To appreciate Webster's words, it is necessary to appreciate the importance which the example of the Roman Republic had for the first generations of independent Americans. The republican heroes of ancient Rome, as known through Livy and other historians, were models of principled republican patriotism in a world that had long been dominated by feudalism and monarchy. A statue of George Washington in a toga was considered very appropriate. Indeed, Washington's favorite literary work was Joseph Addison's play about the Roman hero "Cato." Members of the upper chamber of American legislatures were known as senators, and they met in a capitol building. The model hero for American republicans was Cincinnatus, who left his plow to lead an army in successful defense of his country and then took up the plow again without any thought of using his prestige for personal ambition that might undermine the public liberty. (It doesn't matter that some historians assert that our forefathers did not really understand Rome. The significant point is what their beliefs say about them.)

The notion that Calhoun was all about slavery and nothing but slavery is a product of the current reign of Cultural Marxism, and it does not represent a balanced view of American history. It has not always been so. In 1950 Margaret Coit's admiring biography,

John C. Calhoun: American Portrait, won a Pulitzer Prize. In 1959 a committee chaired by John F. Kennedy named Calhoun as one of the five greatest senators of all time. Calhoun's *A Disquisition on Government* has been recognized in every generation and internationally as among the most important political treatises written by an American.

It is somewhat ridiculous to single out Calhoun as a defender of slavery when no one in his time proposed any serious solution to the slavery question. Indeed, Lincoln himself on his election declared he would not know what to do about slavery even if he had the power, which he did not have. Calhoun was forthright in condemning agitation in the North about slavery in the South, warning that it was threatening the bonds of Union. In the last few years of his life, in response to the Wilmot Proviso, which barred the South from use of the new territories acquired from Mexico, a clear violation of the Missouri Compromise, Calhoun did become the most conspicuous proponent of a defensive Southern unity within the Union. By that time Calhoun already occupied the position of elder statesman, who was admired and listened to by thoughtful people North and South for his adherence to principle and independence of political party maneuvers.

He had been an eloquent and tireless leader of the House of Representatives during the War of 1812, and he was one of the main architects of postwar legislation in which he had shown a constructive spirit generous to the welfare of every part of the Union. As Secretary of War, a thankless post, Calhoun had been one of the ablest department heads ever serving in the U.S. government. He had been elected vice president virtually without opposition and had resigned from that position on a matter of principle. His years of service in the Senate (1833-43, 1845-50) were interrupted by a year as Secretary of State. It is a measure of his stature that when President Tyler nominated him to be Secretary of State, at a time of impending conflict with both Britain and Mexico, Calhoun was confirmed by the Senate in a matter of hours without a single dissenting vote, even from the antislavery senators of Vermont.

Nor was Calhoun a "cast-iron man"—except in principles. His image today is a good object lesson in the proclivity of some historians to resort to cartoon versions of history when dealing with figures they do not like. The description of the "cast-iron" man so often quoted was made by a cranky Englishwoman who met him once briefly. And the

Brady daguerreotype usually displayed to portray Calhoun as a dour fanatic was taken during his final illness. Portraits and commentary offer abundant evidence that Calhoun was a handsome, charming, and approachable, as well as a brilliant, man.

Americans have long been predominantly a pragmatic people, eager to get on with what seems desirable public policy without much attention to principles and philosophy. So that much of what the Roman Calhoun regarded as necessary for the preservation of a healthy republic will seem strange and irrelevant, or even repulsively stern in the twenty-first century. On the other hand, his observations often are those of a gifted prophet who accurately foresaw perils that the United States has failed to avoid.

In 1842, near the end of the session, the Senate was hearing routine committee reports. In a good example of his insistence on republican virtue, Calhoun rose to his feet because of a report recommending compensation to the heirs of General William Hull:

> Mr. Calhoun said that he was not a little surprised. . . . He was, in the first place, surprised that the representatives of General Hull should ever think of presenting this claim to Congress. He would not be more so, if the representatives of [Benedict] Arnold should present a claim for his pay as a general in our service . . . on the ground that he held the commission of a general, which had not been revoked. . . . He could never forget the deep and universal indignation which pervaded the whole country on the surrender of Detroit [by Hull at the beginning of the War of 1812, without firing a shot]. . . . How could his pay as Governor be allowed, when there was, for the time, no such Territory as Michigan? It had, by his own act, become a British province and remained so until it was re-conquered by the army under General Harrison. With what show, then, of justice or equity, could he be paid for governing a territory, that did not exist, and which had ceased to exist by his own act? The error of the committee consisted in supposing that the commission—the mere paper and wax—and not the service, gave the pay.

A similar recurrence to antique republican honor was evoked when the Smithson bequest came before the Senate. James Smithson, a wealthy Englishman, had willed to the United States an endowment for a university. Calhoun observed that Congress in fulfilling the bequest would be allowing a foreigner to empower it to do what had previously been determined to be unconstitutional. "I not only regard the measure as unconstitutional," he said, "but to me it appears to involve a species of meanness which I cannot describe, a want of dignity wholly unworthy of this Government." He continued, "We would accept a donation from a foreigner to do with it what we have no right to do, and just as if we were not rich enough ourselves to do what is proposed, or too mean to do it if it were in our power."

Calhoun believed that government expenditures should be minimal and closely monitored. This belief was unusual in his time and is perhaps shocking to Americans who have long since thought of politics mostly as a jockeying for government benefits.

> We robbed the people in levying taxes. It was plunder and nothing more. . . . Every cent removed from the hands of Government is so much added to the wealth of the people. . . . Every dollar we can prevent from coming into the treasury, or every dollar thrown back into the hands of the people, will tend to strengthen the cause of liberty, and unnerve the arm of power.

This sentiment did not mean that he approved the plans of politicians to "distribute" to the governments of the states a treasury surplus brought about by an unjust tariff. This was not giving it back to the people from whom it had been unnecessarily taken but merely expanding the opportunity for politicians to buy support. In what must be one of the most extraordinary acts of principle in American history, South Carolina refused its share of the unjust distribution.

On other occasions Calhoun called the attention of the Senate to unwelcome truths: "We all knew that when a public building was commenced that it was never finished under five times the original estimate." It was almost impossible to repeal a tax once it had been placed on the books, he said. And whatever the claims of political parties: "All Administrations were nearly alike extravagant. . . . It was impossible to force the minds of the public officers to the importance of attendance to the public money because we have too much of it." "I have no doubt, from what I daily see," said the stern republican, "that our whole system is rapidly becoming a mere money making concern to those, who have the control of it; and that every feeling of patriotism is rapidly sinking into an universal spirit of avarice."

A modern authority on banking and currency, Bray Hammond, has written that John C. Calhoun understood that complex and contentious subject better than any public man of his time.

Characteristically, he refused to be drawn into the party argument between the Whigs and Democrats about whether there should be a national bank or not. He made a deep historical study and his speeches of the 1830s and 1840s on this subject are models of learning and independent statesmanship. Both parties were failing to deal with the fundamental question—who should control the money supply (currency and credit) of the country? The Democrats' Independent Treasury, to do the government's banking business instead of a national bank or Jackson's corrupt system of "pet banks," was a step in the right direction. However, it did not go far enough. The Independent Treasury would continue the long-established government policy of treating the notes of private banks as acceptable money. Therefore, the banking system would retain a large amount of control over the money supply (its expansion or contraction) which meant great power over the whole economy and every other interest. "We must curb the banking system," said Calhoun, once, "or it will certainly ruin the country."

> I do not hesitate to say, if Genl. [Alexander] Hamilton had not issued his circular directing bank- notes to be received as gold & silver in the public dues, and if the Bank of the United States had not been created, the whole course of politics under our system would have been entirely different.

Further, why should the U.S. government, which had a large income, create a national debt by borrowing money from bankers, who thus were paid interest at no risk to themselves? Rather, there should be a complete "divorce" of the government and the bankers. Congress had the responsibility to provide a sound circulating currency for the business of the country. The government should issue its own money, Treasury notes, which, based on its credit, would fulfill this obligation and eliminate the connection with bankers.

When the Independent Treasury came to a vote, Calhoun offered an amendment to phase out the Treasury's receipt of bank-notes. The majority Northern Democrats were not about to offend the bankers and his proposal was voted down. Very seldom has a more fundamental challenge been offered to "business as usual." Calhoun had cut through party polemics to the fundamental truth: the alliance of government and bankers gave control of the money supply to private interests to the detriment of every other interest in society. "It has been justly stated by a British writer," Calhoun told the Senate, "that the power to make a small piece of paper, not worth one cent, by the inscribing of a few names, to be worth a thousand dollars, was a power too high to be entrusted to the hands of mortal men."

As always, Calhoun's ultimate concern was not with money but with the health of republican liberty. He deplored the effects of the banking system on the public morale. The unnatural rewards of banking were diverting able young men from the honorable and useful learned professions and diverting their attention from patriotic service.

Calhoun's warnings about the degeneration of statesmanship due to the development of party organizations and professional politicians were a great source of appeal to thoughtful people in every part of the Union. The Hamiltonians and Jeffersonians had been patriots who had fought over differing visions of America. But the Whigs and the Democrats were primarily election machines. Their campaigns avoided real issues and sought to occupy the noncontroversial middle, to be all things to all men. When the issue was protective tariff or no protective tariff, Andrew Jackson had come out for a "judicious tariff." In 1840 the Whigs elected a president with a noisy and meaningless campaign. In 1844 when the important issue was the status of Texas, the Whig frontrunner Henry Clay and the Democratic frontrunner Martin Van Buren colluded to not mention the issue at all in the presidential campaign, because a clear stand could make trouble for both. Calhoun as Secretary of State disdained this evasion and forced the issue of Texas into prominence. Van Buren thus lost the nomination to a pro-Texas candidate, James K. Polk.

As Calhoun wrote a young friend:

> The Federal Government is no longer under the control of the people, but of a combination of active politicians, who are banded together under the name of Democrats or Whigs, and whose exclusive object is to obtain the control of the honors and emoluments of the Government. They have the control of the almost entire press of the country, and constitute a vast majority of Congress, and of all the functionaries of the Federal Government. With them, a regard for principle, or this or that line of policy, is a mere pretext. They are perfectly indifferent to either, and their whole effort is to make up on both sides such issues as they may think for the time to be the most popular, regardless of truth or consequences.

Calhoun was a vigorous critic of the solidifying system of political party "conventions of the people" to make platforms and nominate candidates. Such proceedings did not represent the voice of the people; they were gatherings of self-interested politicians held together by patronage or the promise of patronage. And they were invariably stage-managed and predetermined by clever professional politicians. "This wholesale traffic in public office for party purposes is wholly pernicious and destructive of popular rights," Calhoun said. The "people individually, have no choice, but to vote for the one ticket or the other ticket. . . . Never was a scheme better contrived to transfer power from the body of the community, to those whose occupation is to get or hold offices."

A twenty-first-century American, contemplating the bottomed-out "approval ratings" of public officials, might be inclined to consider Calhoun as a prophet:

> When it comes to be once understood that politics is a game; that those who are engaged in it but act a part; that they make this or that profession, not from honest conviction, or intent to fulfill it, but as the means of deluding the people, and through that delusion to acquire power; when such professions are to be entirely forgotten, the people will lose all confidence in public men. All will be regarded as mere jugglers—the honest and the patriotic as well as the cunning and the profligate—and the people will become indifferent and passive to the grossest abuses of power, on the ground that those whom they may elevate, under whatever pledges, instead of reforming, will but imitate the example of those whom they have expelled.

On another occasion he remarked that in order for self-government of the people to work:

> It will be by drawing into the Presidential canvass and fully discussing all the great questions of the day. One of my strong objections to the caucus system is that it stifles such discussions, and gives the ascendancy to intrigue & management over reason & principles. It is in fact an admirable contrivance to keep the people ignorant and debased.

It was frequently said by opponents and has been repeated by historians that Calhoun was too idealistic for politics. One superficial historian has even said that Calhoun "was out of touch with reality" during the Nullification crisis of 1831-33, despite the fact that Calhoun and his "gallant little State," standing against almost the entire political power of the Union, achieved a reduction of the tariff.

Such critics miss the point. Calhoun was not out of touch with reality, he simply disdained the "reality" of ordinary political expediency and compromise. He strove to be a statesman. A politician was one who cut deals to achieve and keep office. The duty of a statesman was to acquaint the people with the big picture, with the long-range consequences of seemingly expedient measures. A statesman would foresee avoidable dangers. Near the end of his life, Calhoun solemnly and accurately predicted that unless his countrymen changed their ways, the Union would be disrupted within a decade.

Calhoun strongly supported the War of 1812, which he regarded as a necessary defense of American honor against intolerable provocation. There was much opposition to the war. Calhoun made these sensible and moderate remarks to the House of Representatives on the question of opposition in wartime:

> How far the minority in a state of war may justly oppose the measures of government, is a question of the greatest delicacy. On the one side, an honest man, if he believed the war to be unjust or unwise, would not disavow his opinion; but on the contrary, an upright man would do no act, whatever he might think of the war, to put his country in the power of the enemy. It is this double aspect of the subject which indicates the course that reason approbates. Among ourselves at home we may contend; but whatever is requisite to give the reputation and the arms of the republic superiority over its enemy, it is the duty of all, the minority no less than the majority, to support. . . . In some cases it may possibly be doubtful, even to the most conscientious, how to act. It is one of the misfortunes of differing from the rest of the community on the subject of war.

In monarchies, the decision to go to war was made in the interest of the ruler. But for the United States, Calhoun said, war "ought never to be resorted to except when it is clearly justifiable and necessary." In a republic, war must never be undertaken except when circumstances "will justify it in the eye of the nation." And war must always be undertaken gravely and honorably, without "bullying" and threats "nor the ardor of eloquence to inflame our passions."

It is in regard to foreign relations and war that Calhoun made his most telling and unheeded prophecies about the consequences of violating true republican principles. Calhoun delighted in the expansion of the American people across the continent. It was the very energy and enterprise of the American people that made war unnecessary. Their own unofficial efforts would bring under American control all the territory that could reasonably be desired:

> Peace is, indeed, our policy. Providence has cast our lot on a portion of the globe sufficiently vast to satisfy the most grasping ambition, and abounding in resources above all others, which only require to be fully developed to make us the greatest and most prosperous people on earth. . . . let a durable and firm peace be established, and this Government be confined rigidly to the few great objects for which it was instituted; leaving the States to contend in generous rivalry, to develop, by the arts of peace, their respective resources, and a scene of prosperity and happiness would follow heretofore unequalled on the globe.

The U.S. government had no need for provocative words and acts, much less conflicts with other powers. All the government needed was a policy of "masterly inactivity." As Secretary of State, Calhoun worked toward a compromise with Great Britain over the Oregon Territory, realizing that despite the demands of some for "Fifty-Four Forty or Fight," it would be counterproductive to go to war with the greatest power on earth where there was no possibility to place and supply an army. After much bluster, the Polk administration was forced to accept the compromise settlement that Calhoun had made.

Calhoun's statesmanship never showed better, perhaps, than in his stand on the Mexican War. Texas had won its own independent nationhood, and thanks to John Tyler and Calhoun had become a member of the American Union. Tensions remained high with Mexico over the boundaries of Texas and other matters. Polk, upon assuming office, sent an army force to occupy the barren land between the Nueces and Rio Grande rivers, which Mexicans asserted was not part of Texas. A clash occurred with Mexican forces in the disputed area. When the news of this reached Washington, Polk declared that "American blood has been shed on American soil" and asked Congress to recognize a state of war.

Calhoun raised a lonely voice against the surge of patriotism that ensued. He refused to support the war resolution in the Senate. A border incident did not necessarily call for all-out war, he said. Most importantly, a perilous precedent had been set. The President had in effect initiated a war without waiting for the people or Congress. If this precedent were allowed to stand, it would empower any future president to commit the country to war at will. And so it has been.

We can measure the quality of Calhoun's statesmanship and love of democratic government when we realize that the war was very popular, especially in the South, and when we compare him with most of the Whigs in Congress. Opposed to the war and the Polk administration, they nevertheless voted for the war resolution out of fear of being branded as unpatriotic, and then voted no on all legislation to supply the army.

As the war progressed Calhoun repeatedly argued for limited war aims and against the rising clamor of Manifest Destiny. Let the U.S. be satisfied with Texas, New Mexico, and California and not invade and occupy Mexico. His remarks might apply to the twenty-first-century as well as the nineteenth:

> We make a great mistake in supposing all people are capable of self-government. Acting under that impression, many are anxious to force free governments on all the people of this continent, and over the world, if they had the power. It has been lately urged in a very respectable quarter, that it is the mission of this country to spread civil and religious liberty over the globe, and especially over this continent—even by force if necessary. It is a sad delusion. None but a people advanced to a high state of intellectual and moral excellence are capable, in a civilized condition, of forming and maintaining free governments; and among those who are so far advanced, very few indeed have had the good fortune to form constitutions capable of endurance.

The attempt to create a free government in Mexico would only result in the U.S. installing and permanently propping up by force a puppet government, as the British had done in India. Sound familiar? At this time Calhoun wrote his daughter, his closest confidante:

> Our people have undergone a great change. Their inclination is for conquest & empire, regardless of their institutions & liberty; or, rather, they think they hold their liberty by a divine tenure, which no imprudence, or folly on their part can defeat. . . . We act, as if good institutions & liberty belong to us of right, & that neither neglect nor folly can deprive us of their blessing.

To those of a conservative disposition, Calhoun may seem to be a prophet—the full import of whose warnings are yet to be seen.

Grover Cleveland:
The Last Jeffersonian President

The well-known historian Allan Nevins once wrote that Grover Cleveland "was too conservative to be a great constructive statesman." This statement exemplifies the typical response from modern historians when asked about the Cleveland administrations. To them, his conservatism and lack of dynamic executive authority in following the progressive mold are usually his downfall. Vincent P. De Santis argued that, "While it might be possible to praise his good intentions it is impossible to credit him with any major achievements." And Mark W. Summers probably summarized the sentiment of the entire Leftist historical profession when he said in a 2005 History Channel documentary on Grover Cleveland, "I just wish he had only been elected to one term. I think the second term was a great misfortune to him and the country." No one questions Cleveland's honesty and integrity, and recent historical rankings of American presidents place him in the middle of the pack, but his policy decisions, particularly on the domestic front, drive the Left mad. He was not Woodrow Wilson, Franklin or Teddy Roosevelt, or Lyndon Johnson, and that is precisely why conservative Americans should be paying attention to the often-forgotten Grover Cleveland, the last Jeffersonian to occupy the executive office.

Cleveland was born in Caldwell, New Jersey, in 1837. He was the son of a Presbyterian minister of modest means, and his family moved frequently around New York. After his father died in 1853, Cleveland moved to Buffalo, New York, and took residence with a wealthy and well connected uncle. He clerked in a Buffalo law firm, attended college, and was admitted to the bar in 1859. He was appointed district attorney of Erie County in 1863 and later paid the $150 commutation fee to avoid military service during the War Between the States. He was linked to the Peace Democrats in the North, though one biographer believes he privately supported the War. Though his legal earnings were substantial enough to support comfortable accommodations, Cleveland lived in a boarding house and financially supported his mother and sisters. Frugality became one of his principle traits, and he expected nothing less from government.

Cleveland was elected sheriff of Erie County in 1870 and later served as mayor of Buffalo in 1881. He largely steered clear of politics for much of his life, but the political corruption of the Reconstruction period led him to accept office. (Cleveland never "campaigned" for a public office. He was considered honest and upright and his name was submitted by his peers). He was viewed as a reformer, and he immediately took on the party machines of Buffalo. He worked to eliminate graft and once vetoed a street cleaning bill because the contract would have gone to the highest, rather than lowest, bidder. In his veto message, Cleveland remarked that he regarded the bill as a "shameless scheme to betray the interests of the people, and to worse than squander the public money." Cleveland viewed his role as a negative force in the maintenance of the public trust, for he believed if the corruption were exposed, the public would look on in "abhorrence" at the "schemes" of government. In other words, government was not to enrich those with means at the expense of the people at large.

His performance as mayor led several leading New York Democrats to submit his name as a candidate for governor of New York. He won in a landslide over his Republican opponent. Cleveland solidified his views on executive authority in his time as governor. New York was the pit of political corruption in the 1880s, and Cleveland was determined to return honesty, openness, and frugality to the state government, much in the same way he would guide the United States during his two terms as president. His view of politics was simple. On one side resided the "spoilsmen, little and big, all the disappointed office seekers after personal interest, all those hoping to gain personal ends, and all those who desire a return to the old, corrupt, and repudiated order of things in party management," and, "On the other side will be found the true and earnest men." Cleveland was a veto machine, and his reasoning behind each was essentially Jeffersonian, for each was an attempt in one way or another to stifle the corrupt in the name of the "true and earnest men."

In confronting the worst political elements of New York, Cleveland became a star in the Democratic Party and to the American people at large. In 1884, just three years after being elected mayor of Buffalo, Cleveland was nominated by the Democratic Party for president of the United States. Again, like the republicans of the founding generation, he did not campaign for the job, and he showed a humility and sense of duty that George Washington would recognize. He wrote in 1884, shortly before his nomination, that he had

> not a particle of ambition to be President of the United States. Every consideration which presents itself to me tends to the personal wish on my part that the wisdom of the Democratic party in the coming convention may lead to a result not involving my nomination for the Presidency. If, however, it should be otherwise and I should be selected as the nominee, my sense of duty to the people and my party would dictate my submission to the will of the convention.

Cleveland would ultimately serve two non-consecutive terms as president, the only man to do so, and he was the first Democrat elected president since James Buchanan in 1856. Woodrow Wilson once remarked that "You may think Cleveland's administration was Democratic. It was not. Cleveland was a conservative Republican." Of course, by "Democratic" Wilson meant progressive, but herein lays the misinformation surrounding Cleveland. He was a conservative in the Jeffersonian mold, and thus party affiliation meant little. He repudiated and despised Hamiltonianism and while he considered himself a "reformer," reform to Cleveland meant a reduction in the size and scope of the federal government and a return to the founding principles of the United States. Cleveland articulated his core political principles as thus:

> the limitation of Federal power under the Constitution; the absolute necessity of public economy; the safety of a sound currency; honesty in public places; the responsibility of public servants to the people; care for those who toil with their hands; a proper limitation of corporate privileges, and a reform in the civil service.

This statement mirrored Thomas Jefferson, who said in his first inaugural address in 1801 that a "happy and prosperous people" required "a wise and frugal Government, which shall restrain men from injuring one another, shall leave them otherwise free to regulate their own pursuits of industry and improvement, and shall not take from the mouth of labor the bread it has earned." Wilson may have considered himself to be the heir of Jeffersonianism, but a Jeffersonian he was not; Cleveland was.

Cleveland stated in his first inaugural address in 1885 that he endeavored to be:

> guided by a just and unstrained construction of the Constitution, a careful observance of the distinction between the powers granted to the Federal Government and those reserved to the States or to the people, and by a cautious appreciation of those functions which by the Constitution and laws have been especially assigned to the executive branch of the Government.

He kept his word. Like other Jeffersonian republicans, such as John Taylor of Caroline, Cleveland championed low tariffs, light taxes, minimal debt, and sound money. But by the 1880s, Hamiltonianism and corruption had become entrenched in Washington, so Cleveland resorted to liberally using his veto power to demolish as much of it as he could. He, in fact, vetoed more legislation than every man who held office before him combined. He was only outdone by Franklin Roosevelt, but Roosevelt's veto effort was largely to strengthen the federal government and the executive office. Cleveland used it as a wrecking ball.

One biographer contended that upon taking office, Cleveland "knew nothing about being president and nearly nothing about the great national issues," and he complained that Cleveland had neither a "representative of the farmers" nor "of labor, or of various minority groups." This type of criticism is, again, commonplace among his detractors. Yet, Cleveland knew much about the executive office, and his economic program, he argued, would only *help* farmers and laborers whom he believed were burdened with excessive taxes and a depreciated currency. Protective tariffs forced the laboring class, particularly farmers, to be:

> purchasers and consumers of numberless things enhanced in cost by tariff regulations. . . . The plea that our infant industries need the protection which thus impoverishes the farmer and consumer is, in view of our natural advantages, and the skill and ingenuity of our people, a hollow pretext.

And depreciated money and worthless paper dollars spoiled their purchasing power and reduced the value of their labor. These were not the arguments of a man who did not care for the laboring public. On the contrary, he thought the spoils of government had for too long been placed in the hands of corrupt politicians and industrialists at the expense of the public.

Cleveland additionally contended that a frugal government would help the people:

> It is the duty of those serving the people in public place to closely limit public expenditures to the actual needs of the Government economically administered, because this bounds the right of the Government to exact tribute from the earnings of labor or the property of the citizen, and because public extravagance begets extravagance among the people.

When government revenues exceeded expenditures, Cleveland recommended tax cuts in the form of tariff reduction:

> The public Treasury, which should only exist as a conduit conveying the people's tribute to its legitimate objects of expenditure, becomes a hoarding place for money needlessly withdrawn from trade and the people's use, thus crippling our national energies, suspending our country's development, preventing investment in productive enterprise, threatening financial disturbance, and inviting schemes of public plunder.

When the treasury minted silver at a rate that would ultimately cause hyper-inflation, Cleveland demanded that the practice be stopped. Cleveland understood, as did the Jeffersonians, that government manipulation of the money supply would only benefit "rich speculators" at the expense of the "laboring men and women of the land," who would find that "the dollar received for the wage of their toil has sadly shrunk in its purchasing power." To Cleveland, sound money, low taxes, and frugal government only benefitted the working class. His argument for a sound currency was proven correct in his second term when, at his insistence, the Sherman Silver Purchase Act was repealed. The resulting financial stability rescued the United States from a deep depression.

Cleveland famously vetoed a bill in his first term that would have given aid to drought-stricken Western farmers. In his veto message, he opined that "though the people support the Government, the Government should not support the people." This has become billboard material for the modern Left, and it is often displayed as a fine example of the "abhorrent" political philosophy of the

"Gilded Age." While Cleveland's reasoning certainly does not fit with the modern view of government, it comports with his overall philosophy of frugal, limited, and constitutional government. He stated in the same message that he could find "no warrant for such an appropriation in the Constitution." He was in large part the last American president to view the Constitution as a restraint on government.

Likewise, he vetoed hundreds of pension bills for Civil War veterans and their families on the grounds that they were fraudulent and amounted to little more than unconstitutional government welfare (and had already been rejected by the Federal Pensions Bureau). When he lost the 1888 election to Benjamin Harrison in the Electoral College (but not in the popular vote), one supporter wrote that it was a shame his message had not been better trumpeted, for if given the chance, Americans could have been rescued from the notion "that vetoes of pension to bummers and deserters were blows struck at our country's gallant defenders; that blackmail given to rings of mine-owners and manufacturing trusts was fostering home labor; that the rapidly growing mortgages upon their homesteads come from want of more protection." Cleveland consistently showed "care for those who toil with their hands," but not in the method the modern Left would advance; hence, his reputation remains lackluster among "academic historians."

Cleveland attempted during both administrations to be a unifying figure in a time of extreme political and sectional strife. The wounds of the Civil War and Reconstruction were still raw, and as such Cleveland made a conscious effort to have an inclusive presidency. He wanted to be, in the mold of George Washington, the glue that held the federal republic together. He appointed several Southerners to his cabinet, including former Confederate Col. Lucius Quintus Cincinnatus Lamar, took a grand tour of the South, and warmly recognized Southern contributions to American history. He thought John C. Calhoun should be remembered, for "it would be well if all he did and even all he believed and taught and all his aspirations for the welfare and prosperity of our Republic were better known and understood." He called Confederate Gen. Albert S. Johnston a "great soldier" of "the highest personal character." And though rescinded due to oppressive political pressure from the "Grand Army of the Republic," his order to return confiscated Confederate flags to the South was a gesture of kindness to a defeated people. At the same time, he was friendly with former Radical Republican Henry Ward Beecher (a man who once called Southerners devils) and one time "Red Republican" Carl Schurz.

He also modeled his foreign policy on Washington's Farewell Address. In his First Annual Message to Congress, Cleveland stated, "Maintaining, as I do, the tenets of a line of precedents from Washington's day, which proscribe entangling alliances with foreign states, I do not favor a policy of acquisition of new and distant territory or the incorporation of remote interests with our own." This stance made him unpopular with members of both parties, but Cleveland was unmoved by calls for American imperialism. For example, he refused to annex Hawaii in 1893 after a cabal of American businessmen overthrew the Hawaiian Queen. He labeled the entire episode an embarrassment:

> If national honesty is to be disregarded and a desire for territorial extension or dissatisfaction with a form of government not our own ought to regulate our conduct, I have entirely misapprehended the mission and character of our Government and the behavior which the conscience of our people demands of their public servants.

This was the traditional, conservative, American foreign policy, established by Washington and followed, to some degree, by the first five presidents of the United States, all of whom were part of the founding generation. Cleveland did work to modernize the American Navy, but he did not use the military as a weapon for expansion. As he said in his First Inaugural Address:

> The genius of our institutions . . . dictate the scrupulous avoidance of any departure from that foreign policy commended by the history, the traditions, and the prosperity of our Republic. It is the policy of independence, favored by our position and defended by our known love of justice and by our power. It is the policy of peace suitable to our interests. It is the policy of neutrality, rejecting any share in foreign broils and ambitions upon other continents and repelling their intrusion here. It is the policy of Monroe and of Washington and Jefferson—"Peace, commerce, and honest friendship with all nations; entangling alliance with none."

Cleveland was also a religious man and believed that Christianity and morality were essential for good republican government. He wrote in 1887 that:

A wholesome religious faith thus inures to the perpetuity, the safety and the prosperity of our Republic, by exacting the due observance of civil law, the protection of public order and a proper regard for the rights of all. . . . It will be a fortunate day for our country when every citizen feels that he has an ever-present duty to perform to the State which he cannot escape from or neglect without being false to his religious as well as his civil allegiance.

He said after Henry Ward Beecher's death, "Our pardonable pride in American citizenship, when guided by the teachings of religion, [was] to be a sure guaranty of a splendid national destiny." And when pressed about the education of American Indians on government reservations, Cleveland argued "surely there can be no objection to reading a chapter of the Bible in English, or in Dakota if English cannot be understood, at the daily opening of these schools." Cleveland often invoked God in his letters and openly displayed his religious convictions. He was no closet Christian.

On 28 October 1886, Cleveland officially accepted the Statue of Liberty as a gift from the French people in a rousing dedication ceremony. Ironically, while he was governor of New York, Cleveland vetoed a bill which would have contributed approximately $50,000 to the project. It was an unnecessary public expenditure, but during the unveiling, he called the Statue "a stream of light [which] shall pierce the darkness of ignorance and man's oppression, until Liberty enlightens the world." The Statue of Liberty has since become the symbol of American immigration and, as the inscription states, the perception that the United States is the refuge for "your tired, your poor/ Your huddled masses yearning to breathe free/ The wretched refuse of your teeming shore./ Send these, the homeless, tempest-tossed to me/ I lift my lamp beside the golden door!" Cleveland had a far more traditional approach to immigration, one that had been established by the founding generation. He had no problem with immigrants who wished to assimilate with American institutions, but he feared unrestricted immigration to the United States. "The laws should be rigidly enforced which prohibit the immigration of a servile class to compete with American labor, with no intention of acquiring citizenship, and bringing with them and retaining habits and customs repugnant to our civilization." He condemned attacks on Chinese laborers in a Wyoming mining camp, but at the same time asked for greater restrictions on Chinese immigration. He viewed them as incapable of assimilation. He demanded American

Indian tribes adopt Christianity and learn English, for that was the pathway to good citizenship. In short, Cleveland would be shocked at the modern laxity in immigration and naturalization law, as would most members of the founding generation. To these men, citizenship was a prize to be cherished and it carried substantial responsibilities.

Once retired, Cleveland continued to work for sound money and frugal government by rejecting the leftward movement of the Democratic Party. It was Cleveland who led to the choice of conservative Alton Parker as Democratic candidate for president in 1904, the last time a conservative Democrat won the party nomination. Cleveland modeled his public career after the founding generation. Many of his public statements closely mirrored those of Jefferson or Washington. To him, public service was a duty rather than a station, and while some would call his humility disingenuous, his private correspondence reveals a man who rejected public flattery (he turned down two honorary degrees from Princeton and Harvard while president) and excessive ambition and who in many ways "practiced what he preached." He was the antithesis of the modern politician who spends public money to keep his job and who has no regard for future generations or the public trust he represents. Cleveland closed his last annual message to Congress in 1896 with useful advice:

> In concluding this communication its last words shall be an appeal to the Congress for the most rigid economy in the expenditure of the money it holds in trust for the people. The way to perplexing extravagance is easy, but a return to frugality is difficult. When, however, it is considered that those who bear the burdens of taxation have no guaranty of honest care save in the fidelity of their public servants, the duty of all possible retrenchment is plainly manifest.

If only modern Americans would listen.

William Graham Sumner and "The Forgotten Man"

During a lecture titled "The Forgotten Man" in 1883, sociologist William Graham Sumner said, "We hear a great many exhortations to make progress from people who do not know in what direction they want to go. Consequently social reform is the most barren and tiresome subject amongst us." He proposed to analyze the impact of reform-minded legislation on "the man who never is thought of. He is the victim of the reformer, social speculator and philanthropist." Sumner called him the "Forgotten Man," the "simple, honest, laborer, ready to earn his living by productive work. We pass him by because he is independent, self-supporting, and asks no favors." In the modern age, this forgotten man has been called the "silent majority," the productive class, or simply the average middle class American. He goes to work, pays his taxes, attends church, sends his kids to school, and forms the backbone of society. He does not clamor or protest, but he has been immorally burdened by the "good-for-nothing" through social legislation. In short, "the Forgotten Man would no longer be forgotten where there was true liberty."

Civil liberty, Sumner said, is "the status of the man who is guaranteed by law and civil institutions the exclusive employment of all his own powers for his own welfare." Sumner contended modern reform measures belied reality, and the class warfare championed by socialists and pushed by progressive reformers was in no way based on human nature or history:

> The truth is that cupidity, selfishness, envy, malice, lust, vindictiveness, are constant vices of human nature. . . . But what folly it is to think that vice and passion are limited by classes, that liberty consists only in taking power away from nobles and priests and giving it to artisans and peasants and that these latter will never abuse it! They will abuse it just as all others have done unless they are put under checks and guarantees, and there can be no civil liberty anywhere unless rights

are guaranteed against all abuses, as well from proletarians as from generals, aristocrats, and ecclesiastics.

In a common thread throughout his voluminous writing career, Sumner blamed the "jobbers" propped up by legislation for "extorting other people's product from them." In essence, government reform destroyed civil liberty and crushed the Forgotten Man. Sumner argued that a man could never be in charge of "his own welfare" when,

> The government is to give to every man a pension, and every man an office, and every man a tax to raise the price of his product, and to clean out every man's creek for him, and to buy all his unsalable property, and to provide him with plenty of currency to pay his debts, and to educate his children, and to give him the use of a library and a park and a museum and a gallery of pictures.

This was not a simple attack on socialists and legislation that benefitted the "good-for-nothing people." It was an indictment of state-capitalism and cronyism.

Government in the modern era had become the enemy of the Forgotten Man, because it failed in its charge to protect liberty and the honest producers in society. "The Forgotten Man," Sumner charged, "is weighed down with the cost and burden of the schemes for making everybody happy, with the cost of public beneficence, with the support of all the loafers, with the loss of all the economic quackery, with the cost of all the jobs." Sumner believed the only tonic was liberty. "Every step which we win in liberty will set the Forgotten Man free from some of his burdens and allow him to use his powers for himself and for the commonwealth."

Sumner is, perhaps, the most important forgotten thinker of the late nineteenth century. His works are virtually out of print; his philosophy on man, society, war, banking, and political economy is essentially ignored; and his status as a blistering critic of American society at large is unknown by most American scholars. Also, outside of American libertarians, those who do recognize his name often fail to understand or appreciate his positions. For example, the historian Justus Doenecke claimed that the bedrock of Sumner's philosophy was his attempt to apply Darwinism to societal problems. Doenecke based his conclusion on the works of Richard Hofstadter, who wrote a lengthy study on social Darwinism, and Andrew Keller, Sumner's student and successor at Yale University. Hofstadter wrote that social Darwinism represented the "first principles" of Sumner's worldview, while Keller, in publishing volumes of Sumner's work in the early twentieth century, ignored essays Sumner wrote late in life critical of social Darwinism. Keller buried these later works to justify his support of the theory and used Sumner, who could be confused as a social Darwinist, as his intellectual anchor. This was unjust, but Sumner would have expected no less. He thought all men by nature could be self-serving. History proved his point.

Sumner was born in New Jersey in 1840, the son of an uneducated laborer. His family moved around before finally settling in Hartford, Connecticut. Sumner was admitted to Yale in 1859, was graduated in 1863, and then studied theology in Europe. He returned to the United States in 1866 and was ordained priest in the Protestant Episcopal Church in 1869. Increasing interest in political, social, and economic affairs led him to accept the job of chair of political and social science at Yale University in 1872. He remained in that position for the duration of his life. Sumner gained worldwide attention for his essays on contemporary issues, but he considered his role as professor and teacher more important than essayist. His classes were well regarded on campus and usually full, and he had the respect and admiration of his colleagues. He mastered nearly a dozen languages as well as other subjects in math and science. More than anything, Sumner was a scholar and man of letters.

Sumner did not produce much of note until the late 1870s, but by the time of his death in 1910, he was the recognized champion of laissez-faire, sound money, and anti-imperialism in the United States. He was a first-rate historian and wrote full-length biographies on Andrew Jackson, Alexander Hamilton, and Robert Morris in addition to his political commentary. The common, reoccurring theme in his work, regardless of subject, was an interest in the distinctively American political and historical tradition of "individualism and personal liberty."

In an 1887 essay entitled "State Inference," Sumner argued that:

> The old Jeffersonian party rose to power and held it, because it conformed to the genius of the country and bore along the true destinies of a nation situated as this one was. It is the glory of the United States, and its calling in history, that it shows what the power of personal liberty is—what self-reliance, energy, enterprise, hard sense men can develop when they have room and liberty and when

they are emancipated from the burden of traditions and faiths which are nothing but the accumulated follies and blunders of a hundred generations of "statesmen."

In no way was the arbitrary state, be it ruled by a monarchy or democracy, the American tradition, and Sumner feared the effect the democratic state would have on the American people:

> We have seen . . . what the tyranny was in the decay of the Roman Empire, when each was in servitude to all; but there is one form of that tyranny which may be still worse. That tyranny will be realized when the same system of servitude is established in a democratic state; when a man's neighbors are his masters; when the "ethical power of public opinion" bears down upon him at all hours and as to all matters; when his place is assigned to him and he is held in it, not by an emperor or his satellites, who cannot be everywhere all the time, but by the other members of the "village community" who can.

On virtually every topic, Sumner found challenges to personal liberty cloaked in the name of democracy and the will of the people, and though he was an ardent critic of democracy, his venom was more accurately directed at plutocracy and factional government. Under a system where money can buy influence and the "will of the people" has no constitutional restraint, "The boycotted man is deprived of the peaceful enjoyment of rights which the laws and institutions of his country allow him, and he has no redress." Sumner warned that "plutocracy invented the lobby, but the democracy here also seems determined to better the instruction." Centralization and state power were the enemies of the Forgotten Man. "I therefore maintain that it is at the present time a matter of patriotism and civic duty to resist the extension of State interference." But, Sumner had no hope, for American institutions were "made . . . by men of sterling thought and power, and . . . can only be maintained by men of the same type." They would never be delivered intact to future generations because of the "socialistic and semi-socialistic absurdities" of the late nineteenth century.

War and Empire

Sumner considered war to be the greatest enemy of liberty and the pursuance of war and territorial extension to be repugnant to the American tradition:

> The confederated state of ours was never planned for indefinite expansion or for an imperial policy. . . . The fathers of the Republic planned a confederation of free and peaceful industrial commonwealths, shielded by their geographical position from the jealousies, rivalries, and traditional policies of the Old World and bringing all the resources of civilization to bear for the domestic happiness of the population only.

Sumner lived during the birth of American imperialism and witnessed the baneful effects of the Spanish-American War on American political and society. That war led him to produce perhaps his most enduring essay, "The Conquest of the United States by Spain."

This is a curious title, for the United States, by defeating Spain in the "splendid little" Spanish-American War of 1898, destroyed the last vestiges of the Spanish empire and acquired Cuba, the Philippines, Guam, and Puerto Rico. But Sumner suggested this was a turning point in American history:

> Spain was the first, for a long time the greatest, of the modern imperialistic states. The United States, by its historical origin, its traditions, and its principles, is the chief representative of the revolt and reaction against that kind of a state. . . . We have beaten Spain in a military conflict, but we are submitting to be conquered by her on the field of ideas and policies. Expansionism and imperialism are nothing but the old philosophies of national prosperity which have brought Spain to where she is now. Those philosophies appeal to national vanity and national cupidity. They are seductive. . . . They are delusions, and they will lead us to ruin unless we are hard-headed enough to resist them.

This essay was more than a stinging critic of the Spanish-American War; it was an indictment of neo-mercantilism, of the fallacy that American "liberty and democracy" could be carried by the sword, and of militarism. It was an essay on the historic principles of the United States, of the founding tradition, and of American conservatism. The modern "conservative" reader may not view it on those terms, particularly in light of the adoption of neo-imperialism by the twenty-first-century Republican Party. That reader would possibly conclude this was nothing more than "liberal" dogma and un-American. Sumner contended the opposite.

Sumner argued that the Spanish-American War "was a gross violation of self-government." The American people had long considered themselves to be a "self-governing people" and they "boasted" with pride that they differed in that respect from the Old World. The imperial impulse of the war changed that:

> Let us well be assured that self-government is not a matter of flags and Fourth of July orations, nor yet of strife to get offices. Eternal vigilance is the price of that as of every other political good. The perpetuity of self-government depends on the sound political sense of the people, and sound political sense is a matter of habit and practice. We can give it up and we can take instead pomp and glory. . . . If we Americans believe in self-government, why do we let it slip away from us? Why do we barter it away for military glory as Spain did?

Moreover, the Spanish-American War and American imperialism, in Sumner's estimation, did much to destroy the Constitution and replace it with "a colonial system of the old Spanish type." He wrote that:

> The question at stake is nothing less than the integrity of this state in its most essential elements. The expansionists have recognized this fact by already casting the Constitution aside. The military men, of course, have been the first to do this. It is of the essence of militarism that under it military men learn to despise constitutions, to sneer at parliaments, and to look with contempt at civilians.

The Spanish-American War unleashed this natural course of events and had thrown "the Constitution into the gutter." Sumner asked rhetorically, "If you take away the Constitution, what is American liberty and all the rest? Nothing but a lot of phrases."

Sumner further noted that liberty was not the only American institution in peril since the Spanish-American War. "It seems as if this new policy was destined to thrust a sword into every joint in our historical and philosophical system." Sumner was referring to the American economic system and the impact war would have on American democracy. He was dismayed by the trend toward the adoption of a "navigation system" in America "against which our fathers revolted." The end result of such action would be:

> Constant wars with other nations, which will not consent that we should shut them out of parts of the earth's surface until we prove that we can do it by force. Then we shall be parties to a renewal of all the eighteenth century wars for colonies, for supremacy of the sea, for "trade," as the term is used, for world supremacy, and for all the rest of the heavy follies form which our fathers fought to free themselves.

As for democracy and American "exceptionalism," two catch phrases of modern neo-conservatives, Sumner called these ideas in the wake of the war "popular errors which in time will meet with harsh correction." The United States in the late nineteenth century was a vast, sparsely populated land with abundant opportunities for liberty and success. But, Sumner asked, what happens when this ends? "As the country fills up with population, and the task of getting a living out of the ground becomes more difficult, the struggle for existence will become harder and the competition for life more severe. Then liberty and democracy will cost something, if they are to be maintained." Of course, the American people had long resisted a head-long dive into the doctrines of the Old World, but the war and imperialism delivered the Old World and its institutions to the American doorstep. "Now what will hasten the day when our present advantages will wear out and when we shall come down to the conditions of the older and densely populated nations? The answer is: war, debt, taxation, diplomacy, a grand government system, pomp, glory, a big army and navy, lavish expenditures, political jobbery—in a word, imperialism."

Sumner was more prophetic in his prediction for the future of American politics. "The great foe of democracy now and in the near future is plutocracy. . . . It is to be the social war of the twentieth century." His narrative has shockingly unfolded:

> In the first place, war and expansion will favor jobbery, both in the dependencies and at home. In the second place, they will take away the attention of the people from what the plutocrats are doing. In the third place, they will cause large expenditures of the people's money, the return for which will not go into the treasury, but into the hands of a few schemers. In the fourth place, they will call for large public debt and taxes, and these things especially tend to make men unequal, because any social burdens bear more heavily on the weak than on the strong, and so make the weak weaker and the strong stronger.

Sumner's position is the antithesis of the modern statist positions on American foreign policy. Americans are told soldiers bleed and die to protect American "liberty and democracy," that billions of dollars of military spending are necessary to maintain American interests at home and abroad, and that a strong standing army, navy, and air force are mandated by the common expression of "peace through strength." But Sumner contended this was never the

American tradition and was never in line with American principles. Spain had conquered the United States in 1898 because Americans had succumbed to the sirens of the Old World and crashed upon her rocky shores. Sumner said:

> My patriotism is of the kind which is outraged by the notion that the United States never was a great nation until in a petty three months' campaign it knocked to pieces a poor, decrepit, bankrupt old state like Spain. To hold such an opinion as that is to abandon all American standards, to put shame and scorn on all that our ancestors tried to build up here, and to go over to the standards of which Spain is a representative.

Money, Economy, and Government

Sumner considered oppressive government to be the root of societal ills. He wrote:

> Our fathers would have an economical government, even if grand people called it a parsimonious one, and taxes should be no greater than were absolutely necessary to pay for such a government. The citizen was to keep all the rest of his earnings and use them as he thought best for the happiness of himself and his family. . . . Justice and law were to reign in the midst of simplicity, and a government which had little to do was to offer little field for ambition. In a society where industry, frugality, and prudence were honored, it was believed that the vices of wealth would never flourish.

To Sumner, the "vices of wealth" were more apt to be found in a government controlled by the plutocracy. Sumner did not despise wealth or wealthy individuals. He embraced it. "There seems to be a great readiness in the public mind to take alarm at these phenomena of growth—there might rather seem to be reason for public congratulation. We want to be provided with things abundantly and cheaply; that means that we want increased economic power." But what Sumner dreaded was the machinery of government being placed in the hands of the two polar ends of society, the plutocracy and the proletariat. Each would abuse their power at the expense of those in the middle. Hence, Sumner insisted that "the constitutional republic . . . does not call upon men to play the hero; it only calls upon them to do their duty under the laws and the constitution, in any position in which they may be placed, and no more."

"Doing more" often involved schemes of national economic

planning—a "navigation system" or socialism—two philosophies Sumner rejected. Both, in his mind, were based on the common fallacy that "doing something" was beneficial to the American people at large. Legislation, Sumner contended, was always an experiment, but it should be a controlled experiment tested by fact and analysis, *i.e.*, history and experience. "Blundering experiments in legislation cannot be simply abandoned if they do not work well; even if they are set aside, they leave their effects behind; and they create vested interests which make it difficult to set them aside." Because of his optimistic views of progress and his occasional stinging criticism of American society in the founding period, Sumner often appeared to be a man in the progressive camp, but he was always a champion of solid American principles forged by experience.

Sumner specifically railed against two types of legislation: "legislation by clamor" and "speculative legislation." In the first instance, Sumner suggested that "If a faction of any kind assails the legislature with sufficient determination, they carry their point although the sincere opinion of nearly all who vote for the measure may be that it is foolish, or idle, or mischievous, or crude, or irrational, or extravagant, or otherwise improper." Speculative legislation, in Sumner's opinion, was contrary to American principles and sound government. "Speculative legislation is really advocated by assertions which are predictions, and it is impossible to meet it by arguments which are other than contradictory predictions. But all men of sober thought and scholarly responsibility dislike to argue by predictions." In each case, the government would be hijacked and both were disastrous:

> The point is that this legislation by clamor fits no consistent idea of the matter, proceeds on no rational plan, settles no question, but only produces new confusion and new evils, carrying the difficulties forward in constantly increasing magnitude as the consequences of legislative blunders are added to the original ills.

In short, Sumner wrote that "Among us the legislative machinery can be set in motion too readily and too frequently; it is too easy for the irresponsible hands of the ignorant to seize the machinery; a notion which happens to catch popular fancy for a moment can be too readily translated into legislation."

One of his greatest crusades was against protective tariffs, or protectionism—"the -ism which teaches us waste makes wealth"—and he exemplified the Jeffersonian tradition in this fight. Sumner called protectionism "an errant piece of economic quackery . . . a social abuse . . . and a political evil." In contrast, he defined free trade as "*a mode of liberty*" and pointed to the unregulated free trade between the states in the United States as the perfect example. "Free trade is a revolt, a conflict, a reform, a reaction and recuperation of the body politic," whereas Sumner argued protectionism "is a doctrine or system of doctrine which offers no demonstration, and rests upon no facts, but appeals to faith on grounds of its *a priori* reasonableness, or the plausibility with which it can be set forth." Most importantly, Sumner concluded that protectionism created a political and economic environment where "*the government gives a license to certain interests to go out and encroach on others.*" Tariffs were essentially "speculative legislation" and an affront to good government based on sound American principles. "In a well-ordered state it is the function of government to repress every selfish interest which arises and endeavors to encroach upon the rights of others. The state thus maintains justice." John Taylor of Caroline could not have said it better.

Sumner often coupled protectionism with the schemes of monetary legislation, specifically free silver, and considered both detrimental to the "Forgotten Man." He ardently defended sound money and the gold standard, and he considered "free silver" the path to "fiat paper money." The end result of free silver, in addition to paper currency, would be the very problem proponents of silver denounced. "Wall Street" would be the winner and "main street" the loser:

> Every one of these schemes only opens chances for money-jobbers and financial wreckers to operate upon brokerages and differences while making legitimate finance hazardous and expensive, thereby adding to the cost of commercial operations. The parasites on the industrial system flourish whenever the system is complicated. Confusion, disorder, irregularity, uncertainty are the conditions of their growth. The surest means to kill them is to make currency absolutely simple and absolutely sound.

Underlying every attack Sumner levied against silver, protection, or other "speculative legislation" was a disdain for the fusion of government and finance and the injurious effect these "schemes" would have on the average American. Sumner rightly concluded, as did the Jeffersonians in the early nineteenth century, that the only beneficiaries to such legislation were "the jobbers, speculators, and boom-promoters . . . the 'hustling' type." Cheap money would not be a panacea for farmers, because everything they purchased would be more expensive. Crop prices would go up, but so would costs, thus equaling a zero sum gain. Protective duties would only tax the consuming class to the benefit of the factory owner. The Jeffersonian attack on big banks and corporate welfare was rooted in the agrarian tradition. Sumner was a proponent of industrialization, but his barbs found the same target primarily because the American conservative tradition is sound, honest money. It is the money of the "Forgotten Man," and it is rooted in liberty.

Sumner's critique of American society was a constant hammer against the effects of centralization and poorly reasoned and planned legislation. It was born from the experiences of the American War for Independence and human nature. In that regard, Sumner echoed the words of Patrick Henry in 1775 when he insisted that the "lamp of experience" was his only guide. Sumner went one step further by insisting the liberty must be at the core of every legislative proposal (or lack thereof). He wrote:

> The human race must go forward to meet and conquer its problems and difficulties as they arise, to bear the penalties of its follies, and to pay the price of its acquisitions. To shrink from this is simply to go back and to abandon civilization. The path forward, as far as any human foresight can now reach, lies in a better understanding and a better realization of liberty, under which individuals and societies can work out their destiny, subject only to the incorruptible laws of nature.

E. L. Godkin and the Ideal American

Americans seem to have a fascination with the old adage "my country, right or wrong." This they seem to believe is patriotism. In 1896, essayist Edwin Lawrence Godkin wrote that:

> patriotism has been made by the multitude to consist in holding everything that is, to be exactly right, or easily remedied. A complaining or critical man . . . is therefore set down as a person "unpatriotic" or hostile to his country. He may object to the other party, but he must not find fault with the workings of his government. The consequence is that any man who expects to make his way in politics, or even to succeed comfortably in a profession or business, is strongly tempted to proclaim incessantly his great content with the existing order of things, and to treat everything "American" as sacred. Criticism of the government or of political tendencies is apt to be considered a sign of infidelity to the republic, and admiration for something foreign

The result was a distortion of the American democratic experiment. Office seekers had now devolved to the lowest elements of society and politics had become a business to be managed by professionals. Americans, Godkin argued, had brought this on themselves.

> The present generation of reformers are nearly as eager to abolish the Electoral College and the legislative election of Senators, after a century of experience, as the framers of the Constitution were to establish them. The prevailing desire is to remit the work in both cases to the popular vote. This brings to our notice two tendencies, apparently, but only apparently, opposing, in American opinion. One is to throw as much of the nominating or canvassing or preparatory work as possible on individual men, like bosses and workers; the other is to make the constituency of each important office as wide as possible. The whole people of the Union would like to vote directly for the President, the whole people of a State would like to vote for a Senator, and the whole people of a city would like to

vote for an almost despotic mayor, but few want to take any trouble in creating or arranging machinery for choosing them. The work of "getting delegates" to nominating conventions, and making other preparations for elections, is left to professionals; that is, to men who do little else, and who get a living out of this work. The exhortation of political moralists to "attend the primaries" has become almost a joke among the class to whom it is mainly addressed.

Godkin may well have written this in 2011. He in fact said late in his life that he would like to come back fifty years after his death and see what had become of the United States. He would be shocked. Godkin was a perceptive critic of American society, a firm supporter of economic freedom and sound money, an independent political thinker, an opponent of American imperialism, and a champion of civil service reform. Most importantly, he believed in preserving the old American order, and though he did not arrive in the United States until his twenties, he was more of an American than many of the men who were born there.

Godkin was born in 1831 in Moyne, County Wickow, Ireland. He studied law for a brief moment but was more interested in politics and journalism. He took a job in 1853 at the *London Daily News* as a war correspondent during the Crimean War and achieved some acclaim for his work, both in regard to military matters and social commentary. After turning down a job as editor for the *Belfast Northern Whig*, Godkin set sail for America and arrived in 1856. He traveled extensively in the South and wrote several stories about American life for the *Daily News*.

His commentary on American politics was at times belligerent, at times insightful, and at other times mocking and sarcastic, but never dull. For example, he described Democrat Stephen Douglas of Illinois as:

> a model demagogue. He is vulgar in his habits and vulgar in his appearance, "takes his drink," chews his quid, and discharges his saliva with as much constancy and energy as the least pretentious of his constituents, but enters into the popular feelings with a tact and zest rarely equalled, and assails the heads and hearts of the multitude in a style of manly and vigorous eloquence such as few men can command. There lies in his bullet head and thick neck enough combativeness, courage, and ability for three men of his dimensions. The slightest touch of what genteel people would call improvement would spoil him.

He called New York City in 1858 a den of corruption, graft, waste, and laziness:

> The meetings of the Common Council are marked by slang, ribaldry, and drunkenness, and the members are mainly low Irishmen of intemperate habits, who have been unable or unwilling to gain a livelihood in any honest calling. The population of the city is little more than twice that of Manchester, and the expenditure is seven times greater, and yet it is neither paved, cleansed, nor watched. All the better classes deplore and mourn over this, but sooner than put their shoulder to the wheel by going to the polling booth, they pay their contribution, look after their warehouses, and try to make up for external discomfort by luxury and splendor at home.

Of George Ripley, the utopian socialist who established Brook Farm in Roxbury, Massachusetts, Godkin wrote,

> He was considered by the literary class a model critic because he never found fault with anybody. The critic's function then was considered to be not the promotion of literature or art in the abstract, but the encouragement of any American, male or female, who wished to write or paint. The consequence was that Ripley was, until his death, the idol of all struggling authors and artists. That he was a man of wide cultivation and learning, there is no question, and he would have been abundantly able to play the part of a real critic, but for the fact that his heart was too much for his brains.

And during his travels in the South, Godkin described Southerners as thus:

> As long as one is in the country in the South, and lodges each night with the farmers, one finds numerous compensations for the badness of the roads and poverty of accommodation. It is our hosts' naiveté, prejudices, furious fanaticism; the absurdity of their opinions, and the childishness of their threats and prophecies; their complete ignorance of the great world outside their own State, combined with their frank manners, which make an evening with them pass, if not pleasantly, at least not tediously. What they give you they give cordially and with good will, and it is always the best they have at their disposal. It is only when you reach the towns, and have to put up at the hotels, that you realize in its full force and bitterness the discomforts of travel in a country where that portion of the population which possesses brains and training to do anything well, is almost too proud to do anything at all. There is a notion widely

diffused through England, as well as through the Northern States of the Union, that Southern Americans are fiery, hot-headed men, swift to shed blood, quick in resentment, boiling over with independence, and ever on the watch for slight or insult, in order to avenge it. There is a good deal of truth in this; but if there be, it is not exemplified in the sort of treatment which they undergo at the hands of innkeepers. In all the hostelries of the country one sees "high-toned gentlemen" submitting with perfect meekness to arrangements which in England are only to be witnessed in second-class boardingschools.

Godkin could rightfully be classified as a Republican partisan during this period of his life. He strongly condemned slavery and considered men like John Brown to be authentic American heroes. He did not care much for Southern society, and considered the North to be superior, but Godkin attempted objectivity when warranted. For example, writing in 1863 after the death of Thomas J. "Stonewall" Jackson, Godkin said,

> I have spoken at such length about him because I consider his career the most extraordinary phenomenon of this extraordinary war. Pure, honest, simple-minded, unselfish, and brave, his death is a loss to the whole of America, for, whatever be the result of this war, the United States will enjoy the honor of having bred and educated him. And the Puritanism which made him what he was, in which he lived and gloried, was a hardy Northern plant, and had none of the soft odor of the tropics about it. He was a soldier of the old Cromwellian type, the most perfect that has appeared in our times, and most likely the last we shall ever see. And in these days, when it is becoming almost ridiculous to believe strongly and completely in anything, or to be in earnest about anything, a man of this mould is not to be lightly passed by, even if he had not a tithe of Jackson's titles to solid, enduring fame.

Godkin reflected upon his perception of Southern society both in the antebellum and postbellum world in 1877:

> With them the war is history—tender, touching, and heroic history if you will, but having no sort of connection with the practical life of to-day. Some of us at the North think their minds are occupied with schemes for the assassination and spoliation of negroes, and for a "new rebellion." Their minds are really occupied with making money, and the farms show it, and their designs on the negro are confined to getting him to work for low wages. His wages are low— forty cents a day and rations, which, cost ten cents—but he is content

with it. I saw negroes seeking employment at this rate, and glad to get it; and in the making of the bargain nothing could be more commercial, apparently, than the relations of the parties. They were evidently laborer and employer to each other, and nothing more.

Godkin spent time in Great Britain during the American War Between the States but returned to New York in 1865 and founded *The Nation*, the longest continually running weekly magazine in the United States. His eclectic tastes were evident from the beginning. In addition to politics, *The Nation* carried stories on history, art, literature, and society. James Bryce once called it "the best weekly not only in America but in the world." Godkin used the magazine and his position as editor to further his political and economic causes. The first issue declared that Godkin intended it to be an independent critic of the American experience. He wrote:

> *The Nation* will not be the organ of any party, sect, or body. It will, on the contrary, make an earnest effort to bring to the discussion of political and social questions a really critical spirit, and to wage war upon the vices of violence, exaggeration, and misrepresentation by which so much of the political writing of the day is marred. The criticism of books and works of art will form one of its most prominent features; and pains will be taken to have this task performed in every case by writers possessing special qualifications for it.

He, of course, had Ripley in mind when writing the last statement.

He followed through on his promises, and though the paper struggled financially in the first year, he was able to provide a first-class paper dedicated to political and social commentary. He spent sixteen years in charge of *The Nation*, but left in 1881 to accept a job as editor of the *New York Evening Post*. He became editor-in-chief in 1883 and held that position until he retired in 1900. Godkin was the quintessential independent journalist. Though often identified with the Republican Party, he condemned military reconstruction and the corruption of the Grant administration and ultimately split with the party in 1884 over the nomination of James G. Blaine, a man he characterized as perhaps the most corrupt in the Republican Party. He later supported Grover Cleveland and when the Democratic Party split in 1896 over the nomination of William Jennings Bryan, he became a loyal supporter of the short-lived National Democratic Party, otherwise known by detractors as the "Gold Democrats." It is at this juncture in his life that Godkin's political philosophies were best expressed.

Godkin shared much in common intellectually with John Stuart Mill. He called him "one of the most singular men ever produced by English society." Both men were firm adherents to classical liberal economic theory. Godkin favored hard money and was a consistent opponent of both protective tariffs and the "silverites" of the 1890s. In an article entitled "Panics," Godkin chastised the substitution of hard money for paper:

> For the giving and receiving of gold and silver we have substituted neither more nor less than faith in the honesty and industry and capacity of our fellow-men. There is hardly one of us who does not literally live by faith. We lay up fortunes, marry, eat, drink, travel, and bequeath, almost without ever handling a cent; and the best reason which ninety-nine out of every hundred of us can give for feeling secure against want, or having the means of enjoyment or of charity, is not the possession of anything of real value, but his confidence that certain thousands of his fellow-creatures, whom he has never seen and never expects to see, scattered, it may be, over the civilized world, will keep their promises, and do their daily work with fidelity and efficiency.

Paper, he contented, made men poor and facilitated the economic destruction of society. On the other hand, sound, honest, hard money ensured real wealth and prosperity.

He joined the National Democratic movement of 1896 principally because of the silver and tariff issues. The Sherman Silver Purchase Act of 1890 flooded the American market with more than $200 million worth of silver dollars. Godkin and other supporters of hard money saw this as an affront to sound economic principles. He contended that the Supreme Court, through the famous Legal Tender Cases, had granted Congress:

> a power to make any kind of money it pleased; that it had power not only to stamp and weigh the metal or metals which mankind has in all ages agreed to regard as the only true money, the only safe measure of value, but to make money out of any metal or other material, to issue it instead of the money actually current, to raise or lower its value in the market, and to give it any name it thought proper.

This belied historical precedent and Godkin called them on it.

> The [Supreme Court] judged of the power of Congress in this

matter of currency by analogy. It said that Congress must have the power over the currency as an "incident of sovereignty," which all the old governments have had, and the definition of sovereignty was obtained by observing the practice of sovereigns. Turning to history, it found that all the older governments had depreciated the currency for their own benefit, but I do not believe it found one champion of the right to do it, or that any one of these governments ever publicly claimed such a right for itself. So that we have clothed our Government with a power which no other government has ever possessed in the forum of morals.

In their campaign handbook, the National Democratic Party wrote that every man should receive "one hundred cents" for every "one hundred cents worth of work." Godkin agreed, and charged that the "silverites" were harming the working class they intended to help.

As to protective tariffs, Godkin believed them to be a public and political fiasco. They constituted a destructive hidden tax that no one, neither free traders nor protectionists themselves, was able to realistically quantify. Most problematic was the political corruption tariffs brought to both the state and federal government. Men were too easily bought by the wealthy industrial capitalists for their own gain:

> It has been the American policy from the beginning, and a wise policy, to provide, by paying the members, that the legislatures of the country shall be a fair representation of the plain people who compose the bulk of the population. The bulk of the population has but little money, but is keenly alive to the use of money, and eagerly engaged in the pursuit of it. We send to the Legislature, both State and Federal, men who are generally poor and generally honest when they go there, but not unwilling to be rich if a respectable occasion offers, and are very apt to have their imagination touched by the history and condition of millionaires.

The subsequent vacuum of statesmen resulted in a Congress unable to stop idiotic monetary schemes or much else for that matter. Godkin believed gaining wealth for the sake of wealth had become the American purpose. It had not always been so. This was the corruption Hamiltonianism wrought, and though Godkin spoke highly of Hamilton himself and other Hamiltonians such as Abraham Lincoln, Godkin spent his career attempting to destroy it.

Following the Spanish-American War of 1898, Godkin wrote to a friend that, "American ideals were the intellectual food of my youth, and to see America converted into a senseless, Old World conqueror, embitters my age." Godkin had seen the horrors of war during the Crimean conflict as a war correspondent and had lived through the turbulent years of the 1860s. As editor of the *Evening Post*, he waged a war of his own against American imperialism. He thought the growing clamor of American imperialists to be "like Europe" was a troubling trend. "It is no longer sufficient for a people to be happy, peaceful, industrious, well-educated, lightly taxed," Godkin wrote in 1896. "It must have somebody afraid of it. What does a nation amount to if nobody is afraid of it?"

His newspaper was one of the few New York sheets that did not aggressively pursue war with Spain, even after the sinking of the U.S.S. *Maine* in 1898. He blamed the "yellow" press for the war hysteria and thought Americans should remain sober in this crisis:

> These hundreds of thousands write to their Congressmen clamoring for war, as the Romans used to clamor for *pattern et circenscs*, and as the timid and quiet are generally attending only too closely to their business, the Congressman concludes that if he, too, does not shout for war, he will lose his seat. . . . Our cheap press to-day speaks in tones never before heard out of Paris. It urges upon ignorant people schemes more savage, disregard of either policy, or justice, or experience more complete, than the modern world has witnessed since the French Revolution.

When war was finally declared, Godkin supported the soldiers, but harassed Pres. William McKinley for his duplicitous role in getting the United States involved in the first place. This, Godkin, contended, was un-American. His scathing criticism only intensified when the war was over and it became apparent that territorial gain, not "humanitarian concern," was the real objective all along.

Godkin showed the imperialists no quarter. He opined in 1899:

> We then went to work to buy 1,200 islands without any knowledge of their extent, population, climate, production, or of the feelings, wishes, or capacity of the inhabitants. We did not even know their number. While in this state of ignorance, far from trying to conciliate them, assure them of our good intentions, disarm their suspicions of us—men of a different race, language, and religion, of whom they had only recently heard—we issued one of the most contemptuous and insulting proclamations a conqueror has ever issued, announcing to them that their most hated and secular enemy

had sold them to us, and that if they did not submit quietly to the sale we should kill them freely.

This, in his mind, was never the American way. He privately wrote in 1899 that, "Every one who believes in the divine government of the world must believe that God will eventually take up the case of fellows who set unnecessary wars on foot."

He spent much of his life discussing the "problems of democracy." Though he believed democracy to be the best form of government, he argued it fostered many of the calamities of the modern world, including "free-silver" and tariffs. He considered women's suffrage to be a dangerous cause, for it would double the electorate and add to the already unmanageable voting population. If the legislative halls of the United States were currently filled with men of poor character and talent and demagoguery prevailed as it did, he wondered what would happen when twice the number of voters had to be corralled by scheming politicians and the machines they controlled.

He also questioned universal suffrage. In a lengthy discussion of the issue in 1865, Godkin contended:

> That there is no natural right to share in the government, and that the precise form of government in any given country is purely a question of expediency. That the state has, therefore, a right to say who shall vote and who shall not vote, and has in all ages and countries exercised this right. The possession of it is deducible from the right of self-preservation.

Because of the large number of freedmen in 1865, this issue was of paramount importance. Godkin thought the idea of an "educational test" to determine the eligibility of voters to be a valid proposal, but he wondered if it would work due to the pressing problems of political corruption.

The franchise was something to be cherished and earned in Godkin's opinion. For that reason, he suggested that former slaves should not be given the franchise:

> simply because they are blacks and have been badly treated. I want to have the same rule applied to them that I would, if I could, have applied to white men. But let me say that I think there ought to be in the case of *liberated slaves* a moral as well as an educational test, such, for instance, as proof of disposition to earn a livelihood, or support a family by honest labor.

Such a statement could not be made in modern society, but Godkin viewed some type of check on the franchise as a necessity for good government.

> The mistake which, in my eyes, the radical Democrats . . . lies in their denial or forgetfulness of the fact that the highest allegiance of every man is due to liberty and civilization, or rather civilization and liberty. The possession of the suffrage by anybody, black or white, is but a means to these ends. If the majority in the United States were to vote for the establishment of a despotism or a community of goods, I should feel as much bound to resist them sword in hand as I would a foreign invader.

Writing in the 1890s, Godkin said:

> Unluckily, history cannot be made to order. It is the product of ages. The proper substitute for it, as well as for the spectacular effects of monarchy, in new democratic societies, is perfection. There is no way in which we can here kindle the imaginations of the large body of men and women to whom we are every year giving an increasingly high education so well as by finish in the things we undertake to do. Nothing does so much to produce despondency about the republic, or alienation from republican institutions, among the young of the present day, as the condition of the civil service, the poor working of the postoffice and the treasury or the courts, or the helplessness of legislators in dealing with the ordinary every-day problems. The largeness of the country, and the rapidity of its growth, and the comparatively low condition of foreign nations in respect to freedom, which roused people in Fourth-of-July orations forty years ago, have, like the historical reminiscences, lost their magic, and the material prosperity is now associated in people's minds with so much moral corruption that the mention of it produces in some of the best of us a feeling not far removed from nausea. Nothing will do so much now to rouse the old enthusiasm as the spectacle of the pure working of our administrative machinery, of able and independent judges, a learned and upright bar, a respectable and purified custom-house, an enlightened and efficient treasury, and a painstaking post-office. The colleges of the country and the railroads, and indeed everything that depends on private enterprise, are rapidly becoming objects of pride; but a good deal needs to be done by the government to prevent its being a source of shame.

He listed among the pantheon of great American statesmen Daniel Webster, John C. Calhoun, William H. Seward, and Abraham Lincoln.

These men had long disappeared by the 1890s and were replaced with men whom the public and the corporations could manipulate. The American political culture Godkin perceptively warned against has only continued to degrade in the modern era. Godkin did not want to raise the gates over the moat and retreat to the walls of his castle, but he did think the powerful forces of democracy needed to be managed, else American society was destined to be a shell of its former promise. Godkin was not a libertarian. Government had its place so long as corruption did not rot its core.

Godkin was consistently searching for the ideal American, not in a utopian sense, but in a historical sense. His idealism was not rooted in the far-flung romanticism of the transcendentalist movement or the egalitarianism of Marxist progressives. Godkin's ideal American was rooted in the beautiful, the ordered, and the enlightened past. His American had a rational understanding of human nature and society but was well versed in the classics and history and in economics and art. If anything, Godkin thought the ideal American man should be patriotic in the sense that he loved the American tradition of liberty, whether in economics, politics, or society. Like Sumner's "Forgotten Man," Godkin's ideal American has, due to the forces of democracy he hoped to tame, virtually disappeared.

War and Money:
The Lindberghs of Minnesota

Charles Lindbergh, Sr., once told his son, "The trouble with war is that it kills off the best men a country has." Lindbergh, Jr., the more famous of the two men, never forgot his father's advice, even when the tide of popular opinion was moving against him in the years leading to World War II and the American public turned their back on him for his stand against American entry into the war. Both men had advanced unpopular causes at unpopular times. Charles Lindbergh, Sr., vigorously fought the "moneyed interest" during his time in Congress, and his opposition to American entry into World War I led to harassment by the federal government. His son waged a war against American involvement in World War II and lost, and in the process was ostracized by American society. Lindbergh, Jr., has been called anti-Semitic, a Nazi sympathizer, and un-American. His father is often regarded as nothing more than a socialist Republican with a bone to pick. But both assessments are wrong. These were principled men fighting a principled war in the founding tradition. They were American conservatives.

The Lindberghs were a product of place and time. Lindbergh, Sr., often called C. A., was born in Sweden in 1859 as Carl Mansson. His father fled to the United States in 1859 to escape blackmail and embezzlement charges and brought his illegitimate infant son and mistress with him. He changed his name to August Lindbergh and his son's to Charles August Lindbergh and settled on a farm in Melrose, Minnesota. C. A. had a difficult but typical frontier childhood. As the eldest son, he was required to do most of the hunting for the family. He spent hours alone in the wilderness and formed an independent streak that marked his political career. His time in the Minnesota woods also led to a respect for the wilderness and the agrarian life. Lindbergh called his time on the farm the "happiest" in his life.

Formal education was difficult to come by in rural Minnesota. His father helped form the Melrose school district and later donated an old granary to use as the local schoolhouse. C. A. rarely attended, preferring the woods, water, and farm to educational confinement, but he did have a respect for reading and learning, both of which were taught in the home. He entered a formal academy around the age of twenty and in 1881 enrolled in the University of Michigan Law School. He was graduated in 1883 and was admitted to the Minnesota bar later that year. He opened a private practice in Little Falls, Minnesota, in 1884 and spent more than twenty years there. Although C. A. was happy as a lawyer, politics ran in his blood. His father was involved in various political crusades in both Sweden and Minnesota and this rubbed off on C. A. as a young man. C. A. ran and was elected to the United States House of Representatives in 1906 and served five consecutive terms. He attempted to secure a seat in the United States Senate in 1916 but lost and never again held public office.

C. A. was regarded as an independent Republican wary of the corruption in Washington and in particular the fusion of government and finance. His was an agrarian critique based on Jeffersonian logic. He supported Teddy Roosevelt and other Progressive Republicans, but to many Midwestern farmers, the allure of progressivism was based on the recognition that the farmers who supported the Republican coalition formed in the 1850s had cut a raw deal. The Northeastern interest in the Hamiltonian system—central banking, high tariffs, and promotion of industry through federal subsidies—dominated the party and the Midwestern farmers were left in the dark. They had joined with the Northeast for cheap land and the promise of "free soil" when the Republican Party was formed in the 1850s. They did not know that this would ultimately lead to their political marginalization. Lindbergh accepted government power as a way to correct the imbalances of the Hamiltonian system favored by the Republican Party elite. To Lindbergh, reform meant a return to American principles and the Jeffersonian tradition.

His son, Charles A. Lindbergh, Jr., did not share his father's interest in banking or monetary policy, but he did inherit an independent streak and an admiration for the frontier life in Minnesota. Born in 1902, he was the only child of C. A. and his second wife. He spent many lonely days perched high up in a tree watching the logs roll down the Mississippi. Like his father, he preferred the woods and hunting to school, but he had a genuine curiosity in learning and was very bright. As a teenager, Lindbergh left school and worked their farm in Little Falls, reveling in the opportunity to live on the land. Even in his later years, Lindbergh was always seeking the quiet and fulfillment farming provided. But what Charles loved most was technology. He learned to drive the new "horseless carriages" when he was eleven, and served as his father's chauffer during his long political campaigns in the Minnesota wilderness.

Lindbergh studied up on his college entrance exams and enrolled in the University of Wisconsin in 1920, but he stayed only one year. He caught the flying bug. Lindbergh learned to fly in 1922 and worked as a daredevil pilot in Midwestern "barnstorming" air shows and as an air mail pilot. He received one year of military combat training in 1924 and remained in the air reserves for the rest of his life. In 1927, Lindbergh became the first man to fly non-stop from New York to Paris, a feat that awed the world and made him the most famous man in America, if not Europe and elsewhere. Lindbergh had always been a reserved man, and though he politely accepted his new-found fame, he was never comfortable with the press and the spotlight. He developed a growing disdain for their intrusive forays into his private life.

Lindbergh was married to Anne Morrow in 1929, and after the press hounded him during his honeymoon, he purchased an estate in rural New Jersey and attempted to find peace and privacy in a country setting reminiscent of his childhood days in Minnesota. It failed. His first born son was kidnapped and killed in 1932, an event that the press labeled the "crime of the century." Lindbergh blamed the media for fostering an environment of intense interest in his personal life. In his mind, his son would never have been kidnapped if not for their constant prying. This delicate and often hostile relationship with the press affected his reputation during the years leading to World War II. The media never forgot that Lindbergh despised them. They in turn responded by becoming the unofficial mouthpiece for the Roosevelt administration attacks against his character during his attempt to keep the United States out of World War II. This, more than any other reason, is why Lindbergh has been largely forgotten and his reputation diminished. Objectivity was and never has been the media's purpose.

Lindbergh eventually served in the war as a civilian consultant for Ford and later United Aircraft. Because of his anti-war activities in 1939 and 1940, the Roosevelt administration refused a military commission. Lindbergh, however, was determined to help the cause and eventually saw combat in the Pacific Theater. After the war, he won the Pulitzer Prize for his book *The Spirit of St. Louis* and served as an advisor for the United States Air Force and Pan American Airways. He died in Hawaii in 1974, and though Americans generally forgot his pre-World War II activities, his reputation never fully recovered from the vicious attacks leveled against him by the government propaganda machine. The same held true for his father.

Money

C. A. was regarded as having one of the brightest economic minds in the United States Congress. His positions are often called socialist and though he certainly held views radically different from laissez-faire policy, his criticism of the American economic system was an outgrowth of his distrust for the American "money trust." They would have been called the "jobbers" by William Graham Sumner and John Taylor. He wrote in his *Banking and Currency and the Money Trust* that the goal of "Wall Street" was to perpetuate their own power, either through the party bosses or by persuading the American people that their economic system was beneficial to the American polity as a whole and to American individuals in general. Lindbergh urged Americans to rethink their support for central banking and the "Money Trust." "I am assailing with all the vigor of my life the system of banking and currency that so taxes our existence, and I am seeking to prevent the Money Trust form fooling us into adopting changes that will allow it to retain its power." His was a lost crusade, but one that should be remembered for its potency and sagacity.

Lindbergh defined the "Money Trust" as a:

> man-made god that controls the social and industrial system that governs us . . . He is offended if given or called by his true name, and being jealous of his power, he opposed an investigation of its sources. At the present time he has an almost illimitable influence upon our daily actions and is seeking to increase it by framing new currency and banking laws to suit his purposes.

He called the American financial system "extortion" and implored the American people to arrest their continued plundering:

> Since we understand its (the American financial system) effects, our children ought to look back on us with shame if we permit its continuance. It is not the bankers who have primarily fastened upon us this system of capitalizing our life energies for their own selfish

use. It is the banking and currency system, which we have allowed to remain in operation, and create special interests. The people alone have the power to amend or change it. Therefore we and not the bankers are responsible for the existence of the present system.

C. A. targeted the essential elements of the modern Federal Reserve System in his treatise. These included fractional reserve banking, inflation, and the control of credit. In fact, Lindbergh argued that the "people's money placed in the banks is principally used as a basis for credit and on that credit the banks collect the interest which operates to reduce the prices of what we sell and increase the prices of what we buy." It was this manipulation of credit, Lindbergh claimed, that broke the back of the average working American, the "Forgotten Man." This is where Lindbergh was the most Jeffersonian and traditionally American. These were not "Leftist" or socialist attacks. They were an outgrowth of the American agrarian order and an organic understanding of American principles. Not coincidentally, Lindbergh pointed to the Civil War as the turning point in American financial history. It was here that the Hamiltonian system was permanently rooted in American political-economy.

Lindbergh can be excused for his early advocacy of the Federal Reserve System, if only because the alternatives presented in the early twentieth century seemed far more destructive to American principles of sound money and American liberty than the reform measures he favored. Ultimately, however, C. A. foresaw in the Federal Reserve Act of 1913 the "Creature from Jekyll Island." One day before the bill passed the House of Representatives in December 1913, Lindbergh took the floor in an impassioned plea to reject the measure. He said:

> This Act establishes the most gigantic trust on earth. . . . When the President signs this Act, the invisible government by the Money Power, proven to exist by the Money Trust Investigation, will be legalized. . . . The money power overawes the legislative and executive forces of the Nation and of the States. I have seen these forces exerted during the different stages of this bill.

Most importantly, Lindbergh feared the ultimate result of the Federal Reserve.

> The new law will create inflation whenever the trusts want inflation. It may not do so immediately, but the trusts want a period of inflation,

because all the stocks they hold have gone down. . . . Now, if the trusts can get another period of inflation, they figure they can unload the stocks on the people at high prices during the excitement and then bring on a panic and put them back at low prices. . . . The people may not know it immediately, but the day of reckoning is only a few years removed.

Lindbergh was correct, though it would take almost a decade for his prophesies to be fulfilled. The United States, with its brand new central banking system, was able to fund a modern, expensive war against the Triple Alliance in 1917, a war Lindbergh opposed. The economy crashed in 1920, and though the Warren G. Harding administration took the proper steps to restore economic prosperity in 1921, the tremendous expansion of credit in the 1920s "boom" era quickly led to a hard correction in 1929 known as the Great Depression. Lindbergh had said in 1913 that, "From now on, depressions will be scientifically created." The Federal Reserve—with the blessing of the central government—and the press became two "con men" in a game to entice Americans into supporting a system designed to ruin them at the expense of the "Money Trust." In this regard, Lindbergh has become a prophet without honor. What happened in 1920 and 1929 re-occurred during the housing bubble and massive expansion of credit in the 1990s and early 2000s. Lindbergh was a lonely voice in the Minnesota wilderness in 1913. Americans should have listened then and now.

War

In 1915, two years before American entrance into World War I, C. A. took the floor in the United States House of Representatives and urged Americans to resist the growing call for American involvement in the conflict:

> At no point in the world's history has deceit been so bold and aggressive as now in attempting to engulf all humanity in the maelstrom of hell . . . Sober men and women who measure the conditions with unselfish judgment and suggest sane action are pounced upon by the devils in command of the "hell-storm" in an attempt to have them labeled "cowards" and to force us into war over a standard of false national honor. Many of the highest officers of Government fail to sustain their moral courage for common sense, and add to the confusion of the excited by trying to support the demands of speculators.

This was not a new crusade for Lindbergh. He said in 1914 at the outbreak of World War I that, "It is true that Europe is ablaze and the destruction of life and property is tremendous; but nothing should be destroyed here as a result of the war, so why should we allow the European war to destroy our reason?" And in early 1915, he privately wrote that "It is my belief that we are going in as soon as the country can be sufficiently propagandized into the mar mania." That was the crux of Lindbergh's opposition. He argued from 1914 until the United States finally entered the fray in 1917 that the push for American involvement was little more than a deceitful campaign by the "Wall Street end of the Federal Reserve System" made possible by their "subsidized" partners in the American press. The average American had no cause in Europe and no reason to support intervention.

"This is not a monarch's country," Lindbergh stated in 1915, but he could see a drift toward that type of government based on the actions of the Woodrow Wilson administration. He additionally suggested that the United States could not adhere to the Monroe Doctrine of 1823 and support a war in Europe and Asia. The two were incompatible. Americans did have a duty, he believed, to support the president, but when "a citizen has done all he can to reconcile his views with the President's action and is unable to do so he has a right to follow what he believes to be the right course, not only a right but a duty." What Lindbergh feared most, however, was the political impact of a potential war in Europe. "There isn't any such thing as a war for democracy," he said in 1917, and lamented that "dictators will spring up, perhaps even here" as a result of the war. Wilson and his propaganda machine eventually took notice of Lindbergh's opposition to the war.

As he had done on the banking issue, C. A. took up his pen and wrote a blistering pamphlet on the foolishness of American entrance into World War I titled *Why is Your Country at War and What Happens to You After the War*. Lindbergh wrote in the introduction that he predicted the calamity in 1913 and that he was "as patriotic as anyone." This, he reasoned, mandated that he as "a sovereign citizen" write the truth and object to events and ideas that he viewed as wrong, even if it conflicted with the majority party or mood of the country.

C. A. blamed the war on the Federal Reserve System and the "Money Trust" that controlled it. He cited Thomas Jefferson's warning that "Spending money to be paid by posterity is but swindling futurity." This, he said, "applies not only to national debt, but to all debts." C. A. railed against the amount of money borrowed, spent, and printed by the government during the war and predicted dire consequences for the farmer and the laborer, the "Forgotten Man," as a result of the conflict:

> As things now are, the main thing aimed at by the wealth grabbers is to use us—to make of us mere machines to wear out in producing wealth for them. Our children are to be dragged into our useless places and we dropped into mother earth—"ashes to ashes," "dust to dust," good-bye. If that is all we are for, then God bless the Kaiser, the late Czar, the Kings, "Big Business" and all the "Big Boys" who caused the war. It will at least be interesting while it lasts. If we are made simply to wear out in their service, the harder and the more dangerous our occupation the sooner will our ashes be scattered to the earth, and serve vegetable life better, to bud in beautiful foliage of the grasses, the trees, and the flowers.

On the surface, these statements and other attacks against the "Money Trust" are easily branded "socialism." To be sure, Lindbergh favored the working class and supported strong central authority in the name of reform, but Lindbergh supported independence first and foremost, the type of independence fostered on the land. His "socialism" was a reaction to the destruction of the independent farmer at the hands of central banking and the fusion of government and finance. War greased the wheels. His critique was not the class warfare of Marx. It was a recognition that the American ideals of independence and republican virtue were being destroyed by the political jobbers in Washington and the financial houses in New York.

C. A. ultimately became the target of the central government's war-propaganda machine. The plates of *Why Is Your Country At War* were confiscated and destroyed by the Wilson administration and interventionists in both the Democrat and Republican Parties worked diligently to derail his political career. Lindbergh served out the final few months of his term in the House of Representatives in 1917 and quietly departed Washington. He was discredited and even marginalized in Minnesota. He started several unsuccessful businesses and died while running for governor in 1924 as a splinter party candidate. In retrospect, C. A.'s resolute defense of American principles should be better remembered. He was a reformer, and in that regard it is hard to classify C. A. as a conservative, but if he is placed within the context of Jeffersonian tradition, as a man who believed in the agrarian order and the independent American, then it is not difficult to understand how C. A. was a principled defender of the American spirit. His solutions often drifted far Left of the political spectrum, but his model was the traditional American.

His son's opposition to World War II was, and is, more controversial. After the kidnapping and death of his son in 1932, Lindbergh and his wife settled in Europe and became connected to the Nazi regime in Germany. The Nazis were progressive technocrats and Lindbergh's expertise in aviation was admired by Herman Goering. The Roosevelt administration welcomed the opportunity to have Lindbergh inspect the German air force. At the insistence of the American government, Lindbergh traveled to Germany several times between 1936 and 1938. He admitted he admired the German people and the "vigor" of the Nazi government, but he never endorsed Nazism and he questioned their motives on several occasions. The Nazis awarded Lindbergh the Commander Cross of the Order of the German Eagle in 1938 for his 1927 cross-Atlantic flight. This was not unknown to either the Roosevelt administration nor the American people, but after Lindbergh became the spokesman for the non-interventionists in the months before American involvement in World War II, Lindbergh had to continually defend both accepting the medal and his time in Germany before the war.

The America First Committee was founded in 1940 by R. Douglas Stuart, Jr., the son of the vice president of the Quaker Oats Company. Membership included several prominent Americans, such as William H. Regnery, founder of Regnery Publishing, and Jay Hormel, president of the Hormel Meat Packing Company, among others. West Point graduate and chairman of the board at the Sears and Roebuck Company Gen. Robert E. Wood served as the national chairman of the committee. Their first statement of principles urged Americans to "build an impregnable defense for America" and insisted that "American democracy can be preserved only be keeping out of the European war." They sought "To bring together all Americans, regardless of possible differences on other matters, who see eye-to-eye on these principles. (This does not include Nazists, Fascists, Communists, or members of other groups that place the interest of any other nation above those of our own country.)" Lindbergh was their most famous recruit.

Beginning in 1940, Lindbergh traveled across the country stumping for the committee. He spoke to millions of Americans on the necessity of remaining neutral in the conflict. Lindbergh was not a pacifist but a concerned American who thought American principles would be subverted by a prolonged and bloody war in Europe. He wrote in his diary in 1940:

> war was . . . declared by the weak and not the strong, by those who would lose, not those who would win. The declaration was brought about by something that lies completely outside of logic—by emotion, by blindness, by vanity, by courage, by indifference, by pride . . . by elements which are intangible, unpredictable, and unforeseen.

Lindbergh thought America would be better served to stay out of Europe. "Our interference will do no good in Europe, we should have acted five years ago if we intended to fight; we are not prepared for a foreign war."

His public pronouncements against the war followed a similar line of reasoning. During a speech in California in 1941, Lindbergh urged his audience "to decide the direction your country takes—to peace or war." He hoped the people of the United States would choose peace, for Lindbergh could only see "the downfall of all European civilization, and the establishment of conditions in our own country far worse even than those in Germany today" should the United States enter the war. In the end, Lindbergh believed "the only way our American life and ideals can be preserved is by staying out of this war [and] the only way European civilization can be saved is by ending [the war] quickly." Later during a speech in Oklahoma City, he questioned whether Americans should give up their "birthright for the mess of pottage that is offered us in Europe and Asia today; or shall we preserve for our children the free and independent heritage that our forefathers passed on to us?"

The government's reaction to Charles Lindbergh and the America First Committee would have made King George III blush. Franklin Roosevelt and his Secretary of the Interior Harold Ickes ruthlessly attacked Lindbergh and used the full resources of the central government to crush the America First cause. Their activity stopped just short of being a bill of attainder against Lindbergh and the committee. Roosevelt privately called Lindbergh a Nazi and authorized both the Attorney General and the FBI to investigate both the committee and Lindbergh. Ickes went further. He was perhaps the most notorious member of Roosevelt's cabinet and he reveled in the opportunity to discredit Lindbergh. He kept a record of Lindbergh's activities and publically called him the "No. 1 Nazi fellow traveler" and "the first American to raise aloft the standard of pro-Naziism." Lindbergh and the committee, he said, did their best to accommodate and attract "antidemocrats, appeasers, labor baiters, and anti-Semites." It was Ickes's disingenuous charge of anti-Semitism that has endured to this day as a stain on Lindbergh's character. It was fabricated by the government for partisan purposes. Lindbergh and the American people deserved better.

The historian Wayne Cole concluded in a thorough history of the America First Committee and Charles Lindbergh that Lindbergh was by no means anti-Semitic. The only speech in which he publically mentioned Jews was his famous Des Moines, Iowa, speech of 1941. In it he blamed three groups, the British, the Roosevelt administration, and Jews, for pushing the United States into the war in Europe. He said during this speech:

> I am not attacking either the Jewish or the British people. Both races, I admire. But I am saying that the leaders of both the British and the Jewish races, for reasons which are as understandable from their viewpoint as they are inadvisable for ours, for reasons which are not American, wish to involve us in the war. We cannot blame them for looking out for what they believe to be their own interests, but we also must look out for ours. We cannot allow the natural passions and prejudices of other people to lead our country to destruction.

Lindbergh opponents, both in the press and in the Roosevelt administration, instantly denounced the speech and claimed it proved that Lindbergh was in fact anti-Semitic. But an objective review of the speech can yield no such conclusion, and Cole asserted that Lindbergh's private statements on Jews echoed his Des Moines speech.

Lindbergh knew that by mentioning Jewish Americans he "was entering in where Angles fear to tread. . . . It is so much simpler to brand someone with a bad label than to take the trouble to read what he says." No truer words have been written. The conservative Mel Bradford said in 1986 that:

> All of us know that it is "disreputable" and explosive . . . to complain of egalitarianism, except for the strictly economic variety, which we manage to resist. However, if we continue to commit ourselves to this confusion, not one component of that rich patrimony of which

I have spoken can survive. For equality of condition *que* equality of opportunity will fill in all the valleys and pull down the hills—create a power which in the name of all good purposes will be enabled in all cases whatsoever to do with us as it will. Those who wish to follow that broad road to Zion (or perdition) may do so. There is a safety and an accommodation with the powers in such choices. You will not be called "insensitive" or "racist" or "cruel." Your position will be respectable (as the enemy defines respectability), but not conservative, as any of our Fathers would have understood the word.

Lindbergh was that type of conservative. He was offered respectability by Ickes and others in the Roosevelt administration if he would simply back down. He refused because of his principles. Both he and his father shared that type of American independence. They should both be remembered not as modern neoconservatives would like, as a socialist and anti-Semite respectively, but as principled men bent on maintaining the traditional American order of independence and freedom, both at home and abroad.

H. L. Mencken as Conservative

There never has been and doubtless never will be again anyone quite like Henry Louis Mencken (1880-1956), the Sage of Baltimore. His impact on American consciousness and his literary output are so vast as to make a complete treatment and a simple characterization impossible. Local and national reportage, essays on every subject imaginable, literary and music criticism, fiction, fantasy, satire, and serious scholarship in his multi-volume study of *The American Language,* barely begin to describe his oeuvre. All show an indomitable personality, a uniquely strong and independent mind, and an unfailing if often cruel sense of humor.

Mencken, of course, is not forgotten. But recent biographies and the publication of his diaries have diminished the attention and acclaim that he once enjoyed among conventional liberal thinkers for his savage ridicule of the American masses, the "Booboisie." It has become clear that Mencken was no conventional leftist critic of society. This should be no surprise, since Mencken publically treated the great "progressive" figures of his time quite as ruthlessly as he did other politicians and social leaders. The real Mencken, nevertheless, seems to have been discovered by many with dismay. This would not have surprised Mencken, who often ridiculed the shallowness of fashionable thinkers.

Mencken can be understood better when we remember that he attended no elite university, was hugely self-educated, and went straight to work at the age of nineteen as a newspaper reporter. A reporter sees a great deal of life up close, much of it bad. And viewing prominent politicians, educators, generals, judges, and clergymen first-hand does not necessarily improve one's opinion of them. Few writers have ever had as broad an experience of American life, high and low, as did Mencken. Such experience is bound to engender a certain amount of cynicism. (Mencken was never quite as cynical and anti-social as he pretended. He was always chivalric to women, in person and in print, relentlessly condemned lynching and the Ku Klux Klan, and carried on a long campaign for the freedom of Eugene V. Debs, the Socialist leader jailed by Woodrow Wilson for anti-war opinions.)

Mencken covered nearly every national political-party convention of his time. As an objective observer with historical perspective, but without any emotional commitment to a candidate or any expectation of reward, he saw such events realistically for what they are: ridiculous carnivals for dupes while those in the know made their deals in the back rooms. Memorably, he destroyed the mystique of government:

> The state—or, to make the matter more concrete, the government—consists of a gang of men exactly like you and me. They have, taking one with another, no special talent for the business of government; they have only a talent for getting and holding office. Their principal device to that end is to search out groups who pant and pine for something they can't get, and to promise to give it to them. Nine times out of ten that promise is worth nothing. The tenth time it is made good by looting A to satisfy B. In other words, government is a broker in pillage, and every election is a sort of advance auction sale of stolen goods.

Some of Mencken's contrary conservatism and independence of mind is also probably due to the fact that, unlike nearly all the prominent liberal intellectuals of his time, Mencken grew up in the Southern-influenced city of Baltimore. His "Sahara of the Bozart" article, which dismissed the American South as a land utterly devoid of culture, is well-known. (Not for the only time, Mencken exaggerated. At the time he wrote this article, William Faulkner and the Southern Agrarians were already waiting in the wings.) Less well known is the fact that Mencken regarded the Civil War as a victory of Babbitts over gentlemen. Nearly everything that Mencken found wrong with American politics and culture, which was a lot, and his disdain for "democracy" as the rule of inferior men over their betters, can be summed up as Babbittry—the absence of any aristocratic leavening in society.

"My own native town of Baltimore," he wrote, "was greatly enriched . . . both culturally and materially" by ex-Confederates who made it their home after the war. If Baltimore was "less corrupt today than most other large American cities, the credit belongs largely to Virginians, many of whom arrived with no baggage save good manners and empty bellies." Mencken was less than conventionally respectful of Lincoln, and commented that the Gettysburg Address, though beautiful, was the opposite of truthful.

Without a leavening of genuine aristocrats, men of strong personal honor, democracy could only sink to the lowest common denominator, thus "the catastrophe of Appomattox." The "Vanderbilts, Astors, Morgans, Garys, and other such earls and dukes of the plutocracy" could never fill the bill: "their culture, like their aspiration, remains that of the pawnshop." Perhaps even Mencken would be surprised to learn that plutocrats like the Rockefellers, Kennedys, and Bushes have established dynasties in politics, a field which they had previously been content to leave with lesser men. In a country with almost 37 million eligible native-born white adults, many of them wise, democracy could only "pick out a Coolidge to be the head of State." It was as though a man offered a sumptuous banquet "should turn his back upon the feast and stay his stomach by catching and eating flies."

It is also true that a great satirist like Mencken is necessarily a conservative, for a satirist is the upholder of values, a chronicler of the gap between what is and what ought to be. For a cultivated man with high standards, the shallowness of culture, politics, and religion that Mencken witnessed in the early part of the twentieth century was catastrophic. It was a long way down from Washington and Jefferson to Chester Arthur and Warren Gamaliel Harding. To victims of his pen who complained about his lack of "constructive criticism," Mencken replied that a critic and a reformer were two very different things. A critic tells the truth without any expectation of reform of the un-reformable. All a critic could do was enjoy the spectacle.

Mencken took no prisoners in his treatment of the Republican luminaries of his day like Harding, Coolidge, Hoover, and Henry Cabot Lodge, or Democratic populists from the boondocks like William Jennings Bryan. But he was just as biting with liberal heroes like Woodrow Wilson and the two Roosevelts. These change agents have become American icons, who must be bowed down to by all right-thinking people of any party. Not so for Mencken. To read what he had to say about them before hagiography had become hardened is very illuminating. And though Mencken characteristically exaggerates, what he has to say about these figures, who were, after all, only flawed human beings like all the rest of us, is true enough to dissolve any unthinking hero worship.

Teddy Roosevelt he compared to Kaiser Wilhelm for his strutting and militarism. Mencken pointed out the phoniness and inconsistencies in T. R.'s positions, and his posturing and mock-heroic rhetoric, which often became ludicrous. When we remember that Teddy Roosevelt was our first celebrity president, that he was in many ways a strange and warped man, and that he changed the image of the presidential office in ways not always for the better, we must give Mencken credit for his clarity of observation.

Woodrow Wilson, the erstwhile defender of democracy, reformer, and peacemaker, was the embodiment of everything that Mencken despised in American life. Rather than the New Freedom, the "Archangel Woodrow" had created the New Euphuism. Mencken's critique of Wilson's "scholarly" writing is unforgiving and all too true:

> Its ideational hollowness, its ludicrous strutting and bombast, its heavy dependence upon greasy and meaningless words . . . an almost inexhaustible mine of bad writing, faulty generalizing, childish pussyfooting, ludicrous posturing and naïve stupidity. To find a match for it one must try to imagine a biography of the Duke of Wellington by his barber.

Wilson as a politician, besides personally being a malicious and egotistical Puritan hypocrite, was an expert at "the great task of reducing all the difficulties of the hour to a few sonorous and unintelligible phrases, often with theological overtones." His popularity rested on his talent in "how to arrest and enchant the boobery with words that were simply words, and nothing else." Further: "reading his speeches in cold blood offers a curious experience. It is difficult to believe that even idiots ever succumbed to such transparent contradictions, to such gaudy processions of mere counter-words, to so vast and obvious a nonsensicality." Mencken was, of course, describing speeches that many then and later received as commanding wisdom about America's nature and its role in international affairs.

Tracing Mencken's commentary through the twelve years of Franklin D. Roosevelt's presidency allows us to put together a pretty clear picture of Mencken's mature political inclinations. In 1932 he announced that he was voting for FDR, about whom he expressed a cautious optimism. Compared to most of his predecessors, Roosevelt appeared to be something of a gentleman, intelligent, and possessed of a sense of humor. Mencken was under no illusions about the not-always-comely wheeling and dealing that had got FDR the nomination.

In Roosevelt's early statements, seeming to suggest a mobilization of all society under the federal government, Mencken thought he detected a whiff of fascism. This was a feeling shared by many and not surprising considering currents in Europe at the time. For Mencken, it began a process of gradual disappointment and disillusionment that led him to conclude by 1936 that the New Deal was just one more political racket and to refer to FDR as "Roosevelt Minor." By 1933 Mencken was writing of FDR: "The only will left in the national government is his will. To all intents and purposes he is the state." The difficult state of affairs confronting the United States at that time prompted Mencken to offer a "simple suggestion." A Constitutional convention might be called to "consider the desirability of making Dr. Roosevelt King in name as well as fact." FDR could then concentrate on improving the state of affairs without the distractions of leading a schizophrenic party, passing out patronage, and planning for reelection. Mencken, who, at least at times, was fundamentally an old states' rights, limited-government Democrat, insisted, of course, that such a monarchy would have to be carefully defined constitutionally. Many times in his political commentary Mencken warned against the temptation to dictatorship whether from the Right or the Left. Dictatorship might at first seem attractive to many, especially the dispossessed. But it always ended in "rough usage for multitudes" of decent men. In the second year of Roosevelt's reign, Mencken observed, perhaps shrewdly:

> About some of Dr. Roosevelt's schemes to save us all from ruin, revolution and cannibalism there are rising doubts, but the popularity of the man himself continues. . . . In part this is due to his sheer skill as a politician, or as one would say if he were not President of the United States, as a demagogue, but probably a large part is due to a widespread and not irrational confidence in his intelligence and courage. We have had so many Presidents who were obvious numskulls that it pleases everyone to contemplate one with an active cortex, and so many who hugged their corners that it is stimulating to have one who leaps out into the ring, and can give as well as take.

The New Deal did not work—it did not save the economy and

restore prosperity. One of the aspects that worried Mencken the most is what we call "entitlements," though he did not use the word, and will seem prophetic to later times. Various segments of society were being addicted to perpetual government support. Such addictions were impossible ever to overcome and they promised eventually a catastrophic government debt.

The last national convention that Mencken reported, a few months before the stroke that ended his writing career, was that of the Progressive Party that nominated Henry A. Wallace for president in 1948. In a piece called "The Wallace Paranoia," Mencken described this event as "swarms of crackpots" and a "street convention of reformers," all being manipulated by Communists.

> Such types persist, and they do not improve as year chases year. They were born with believing minds, and when they are cut off by death from believing in an F.D.R., they turn inevitably to such Rosicrucians as poor Henry. . . . The believing mind reaches its perihelion in the so-called Liberals. They believe in each and every quack who sets up his booth on the fair-grounds, including the Communists. The Communists have some talents too, but they always fall short of believing in the Liberals.

Many of Mencken's opinions seem today dated, mistaken, or excessive—his scientific materialism and dismissal of religion, his big city distaste for the plain folk of the Heartland, his preference for Germany over Britain and disdain for "the Anglo-Saxon," and his championship of bad writers like Theodore Dreiser. However, what he had to say about the shortcomings of American politics and culture, alas, rings even truer in this present century than it did in the twentieth century. It is unlikely, however, that today's American discourse would permit a Mencken. Now he would be brought before the bench and hustled off for compulsory sensitivity training.

James Gould Cozzens: Conscience, Duty, and Love

When we hear a reference to the "American conscience" these days, we usually think of a collective phenomenon. The "American conscience" tends to be invoked whenever some reformer has discovered a supposed evil in society that must be eradicated by government action. (It usually involves correcting *other* people and psychic and/or financial profit to the reformer.) James Gould Cozzens, by contrast, was a writer whose fictional world dealt with conscience in a traditional way—as the struggle of decent individuals to do what is right in the imperfect world around them. Though deeply engaged with questions of moral responsibility, Cozzens is never preachy or sentimental. In his world love is tough. In his books, as in life, doing the right thing sometimes involves discovering and embracing a lesser evil, or taking a sacrificial responsibility for others that is unwanted, unappreciated, or even unknown.

Cozzens's most important works were published in the 1940s and 1950s, a time when writers like John Steinbeck, Norman Mailer, Jack Kerouac, and others were celebrated for purveying the seamier underside of American life. Cozzens, however, was concerned with normal Americans. (He was once quoted as saying he could not read ten pages of Steinbeck without throwing up.) Cozzens's disdain for fashionable liberal concerns and sympathetic portrayal of Old Stock Americans made him anathema, of course, to the New York literary establishment, which routinely labeled him as "reactionary." It did not help that he did not give interviews, avoided publicity as well as all literary society and politics, and lived in out-of-the-way places that nobody had ever heard of.

As a result Cozzens remains semi-forgotten, though he was, as the most discerning critics have avowed, a far greater writer than many of his better-known contemporaries. One recent sympathetic conservative writer has described Cozzens as "the voice of the

WASP." This is true but is condescending and wholly insufficient in assessing Cozzens's achievements.

Cozzens was born in 1903 and died in 1979 at the age of seventy-four, long past the time of his most significant works. He grew up mostly in New York suburbs and among the upper-middle-class Americans of the Northeast that he wrote about. His forebears on both sides were of the very earliest New England settlers and were long prominent and prosperous. He attended the Episcopal Kent School in Connecticut. However, the early and sudden death of his father apparently created financial problems. Cozzens dropped out of Harvard after his second year and thereafter worked at various jobs for his living. Not until the eve of World War II did his struggle for recognition as a writer begin to show signs of success.

World War II was the exception to Cozzens's quiet private life. He served on the staff of Gen. Henry H. Arnold, commander of the army air forces, rising to the rank of major. His job was to run interference between his general and the press, requiring him to be extremely well informed about a host of matters and to exercise immense discretion. This experience was put to good use in *Guard of Honor*, perhaps his second-best book.

While Cozzens is concerned usually with people in moral dilemma, his characters are never the "alienated" individuals of modernist fiction. Like all real human beings, and like the characters in all worthwhile literature, they are people enmeshed in communities, interconnected, for better or worse, with those around them. *The Last Adam* (1933) concerns a small town doctor. *Men and Brethren* (1936), an under-rated masterpiece, portrays the tribulations of one day in the life of an Episcopal minister, and *The Just and the Unjust* (1942) describes a lawyer's ethical challenges.

The description of these early works might make Cozzens's books seem more formulaic than they are. In Cozzens's major works, there is a central character, usually an upper-middle-class Old Stock American in a grave and unexpected crisis. But there is also a dense collection of very real people in the surrounding community, not all of them WASPS, suffering the very real problems and sorrows of the human condition. Though Cozzens was faulted for not dealing with problems in fashionable liberal ways, he by no means avoided reality, as was sometimes charged. Troubled marriages, domestic abuse, infidelity, unwed pregnancy, abortion, alcoholism, physical disability, depression, suicide, financial hardship, racial tension, over-indulgent parents and ungrateful children, disloyalty and betrayal, grave and insoluble problems of professional ethics, the challenges and losses of war, and much else appear—as human problems rather than social causes.

It is not difficult to see why Cozzens was *persona non grata* in the leftist literary culture of the 1930s. In *Men and Brethren* a seasoned clergyman tells a young radical one who had complained of social injustice:

> Your friends downtown aren't getting anywhere, Wilber. They're sentimentalists. They don't believe in the doctrine of original sin. Realists are the only people who get things gone. Don't waste your time trying to change things so you can do something. Do something, do your Christian duty, and in time you may hope things will change.

In *Guard of Honor* (1948) Cozzens's fiction reached outstanding maturity. It received his only Pulitzer Prize and has been called by some the premier American novel of World War II. The central plot concerns Norman Ross, an aging judge, in uniform for the duration. Ross is chief of staff to a brilliant young general of air forces who is making large, complex, and vital preparations for winning the war. Ross must guard his chief against distractions and pitfalls created by bureaucracy, rivalry, misunderstanding, and human error and cussedness. To do so he must navigate relentless problems with the softness of a dove and the wiliness of a serpent, all the while keeping his eye on the essential goal.

The novel takes place over only three days at a home-front military base. Besides the main characters, a host of other normal and believable Americans appear until the reader feels he has a realistic and memorable picture of his countrymen (and country women) living out the unfamiliar and hard experience of mobilization for total war.

By Love Possessed (1957) is probably Cozzens's best contribution to the portrayal of normal American life in his time, as well as a moving treatment of the human condition. It was his most (and last) commercially successful work. *By Love Possessed* struck the heart of general readers, achieving number one best-seller status. It was made into a major Hollywood movie starring Thomas Mitchell, Jason Robards, Lana Turner and other well-known stars. (Surprisingly, the film, although it takes some liberties with the plot, preserves the book's central theme.)

By Love Possessed is set in an ordinary old-fashioned and stable small city of a type that used to be common. Many of its interrelated people are "possessed by love" of various sorts, nourishing or unhealthy, or wounded by the lack of it. Arthur Winner has long been the most prominent and trusted lawyer in town, but his powers are now failing. Gradually, along with his two younger partners, we learn that Winner has been for years carrying a heavy secret burden. The Depression killed off a major local industry, destroying the modest investments of many citizens. Winner has been continuing to pay dividends from the failed company to widows and orphans and local charities. He does so by constantly moving around the funds in his keeping. This is, of course, entirely illegal and certainly disastrous if exposed. It requires intricate planning, clandestine record-keeping, and ceaseless maneuvering in addition to unrelenting vigilance to outsmart judges and slick big city lawyers.

The two younger partners, although each is facing a personal crisis, realize that they must take up, carry on, and live with the burden they have discovered. They have a duty that must be performed, for they too are possessed by love—for their mentor and for their community. It is an unselfish love inseparable from an archaic sense of duty.

The works of James Gould Cozzens are perhaps the best guides in our literature to American life and character in that vanished period just before the catastrophe of moral and cultural breakdown and government aggrandizement that we know as the sixties.

Citizen Faulkner: "What We Did, In Those Old Days"

William Faulkner is of course a giant of twentieth-century literature. Study of his works of fiction is an immense and worldwide scholarly industry. Most of the vast published commentary is academic effluvia without much usefulness in understanding who Faulkner was and what he really thought about the twentieth-century America that he lived in. Conventionally, Faulkner has been described as a Southern liberal. To the liberal academic, it is inconceivable that so great a mind could be anything else. But then there are a few examples of liberal "scholars" whose work consists of a breathless discovery that Faulkner, alas, was not a liberal, and therefore not as smart or as noble in character as themselves.

We should be clear that the essential and important thing about a great artist is his vision, not his opinions. A great artist sees in ways far more fundamentally true and meaningful than mere opinion. Faulkner's political and social views are secondary to his vision. In twelve major works, more than half of them masterpieces, he has presented a panorama of American experience in the nineteenth and twentieth centuries in relation to nature, God, and history that will last as long as Western Civilization. Such an artist is inspired, and inspiration in its root meaning is something that comes from the gods. Even so, to understand Faulkner's opinions as a man when he is speaking for himself and not though a character is one clue to understanding his works.

Fortunately we have the wisdom of several great scholars (something as rare as a great writer) to guide us in understanding what Faulkner is about—where he is coming from, as they say. Most notably Cleanth Brooks, author of *William Faulkner: The Yoknapatawpha Country; William Faulkner: Toward Yoknapatawpha and Beyond;* and *On the Prejudices, Predilections, and Firm Beliefs of William Faulkner;* and James B. Meriwether, editor of *William Faulkner: Essays, Speeches, and Public Letters.*

Faulkner's novel *The Reivers* begins with the words "Grandfather said . . .," followed by a discussion of a gentleman's responsibilities and how he should behave. In most any modern novel, as M. E. Bradford points out, such a discussion would be ironic, the object of ridicule. Faulkner is capable of some of the most uproarious humor in modern fiction, and indeed what follows in *The Reivers* is a hilarious account of what can happen when Grandfather's instruction is not heeded. However, the advice itself is not a joke.

In *Go Down, Moses* the character Ike McCaslin usually has been taken to be an admirable figure. He repudiates his family inheritance because it is tainted with slavery and miscegenation, and he makes his living with his hands. He is a model liberal devoted to justice and repudiation of social evil. But look more closely. One sees that McCaslin is a barren man, driven by an overly fastidious and abstract conception of good. He has no children; his wife draws no comfort from him. He is everybody's uncle and loved by nobody. The real hero is the flawed and worldly Cass Edmonds, who accepts who he is, takes hold of the tarnished family bequest, and does his best to carry out responsibilities to his people, black and white. This is what Faulkner's so often misunderstood vision of life is telling us.

This was not written by an alienated, self-appointed superior "artist" criticizing his society from outside. This is the work of a man who belongs, who is loyal to his people, and who understands that, like all us human creatures, they struggle constantly and not always successfully with sin.

It is clear here and elsewhere that Faulkner admires and believes in honor, or chivalry, if you will. He shows the evil and futility of chivalric pride and violence, but at the same time provides us sterling portraits of courage and honor informed by Christian virtues and in service to community. The most conspicuous example is perhaps at the end of *The Unvanquished,* when Bayard Sartoris faces down his father's killer unarmed in order to stop the cycle of violence spawned by the war and "Reconstruction." Then there is Gavin Stevens who, through several novels and stories devotes himself quietly (and quixotically) to the people of Yoknapatawpha, and at least once is even referred to as a "knight."

There are plenty of bad people in Faulkner's work, though they are usually tragic rather than villainous. But ordinary folk often provide us with unexpected and quiet examples of honor, courage, and sacrifice. Grandmother Rosa Millard finds a way to trick the

Yankees and feed the war-ravaged people of Yoknapatawpha even though it is dangerous and requires sacrifice of lifelong honesty. A convict, temporarily released in order to help in the great flood, finds a new life but returns to finish his sentence so that his new life can begin clean. In "Two Soldiers" a farm boy so poor he has to listen to the radio outside a neighbor's window leaves for Memphis to enlist the day after Pearl Harbor. In *Intruder in the Dust,* an old lady and a boy face down the community to save a wrongly accused black man—even though the man is cantankerous and ungrateful.

It is worth remembering that before the cultural catastrophe of the sixties, Faulkner and other significant writers actually reached millions of middle-class households every week in the *Saturday Evening Post.*

Faulkner in his own life was an exemplar of honor in several respects. "Faulkner's great courage and patience and unceasing productivity are inspiring," writes George Garrett. "The absence of recognition and reward did not silence him, nor did his belated triumph." And through a lifetime of reaching new horizons in his craft, Faulkner struggled to make a living and fulfill his private responsibilities. His Nobel Prize Address, one of the noblest short speeches of the twentieth century, is an exercise of chivalry. To a generation rising to maturity in the early 1950s under a nuclear cloud, for the first time in history, he offers a sober Christian hope and reaffirms the essential meaningful continuity of man's life on this planet.

Cleanth Brooks convinces us that Faulkner was no alienated liberal exposer of an evil society by demonstrating beyond doubt that the central character of all his work is his "community," the "little postage-stamp of land" in Mississippi that he has rendered in fiction as the town of Jefferson and the county of Yoknapatawpha. "The past is not dead," says the Mississippi storyteller, "It is not even past." This is Edmund Burke's sentiment that true community exists in the relationship between the dead, the living, and the unborn. Faulkner is no alienated critic, he is that archaic thing: a bard who records and celebrates the life of his people. What could honor continuity better than the lady who must make the hazardous journey from Carolina to frontier Mississippi in the early nineteenth century who takes with her the stained glass from the doorway and rose cuttings from the old home?

Faulkner's community is a rich panorama embracing the

generations, the rich and poor, good and bad, and the red, white, and black living out their times in the eternal struggle that he describes in the Nobel speech. Life is full of uncertainty and pain, but man, made in the image of God, "will not only endure, but prevail."

It is little known, but William Faulkner has in fact left us with a clear guide to his opinions. When he passed away he was working on a non-fiction book to be called "The American Dream—What Happened To It?" Enough survives to show what was intended. In 1952, the year after the Nobel address, Faulkner was invited to speak to a meeting of farmers at Cleveland, Mississippi. He chose as his topic the Declaration of Independence.

The noble American principle of a right to life, liberty, and the pursuit of happiness, Faulkner said, had become in postwar American society little more than a short-hand for material security. The "American Dream" had become two cars, a swimming pool, and a Caribbean vacation. That is not what the pursuit of happiness meant to the early Americans—people who made the dangerous ocean voyage to an unknown continent, repeatedly penetrated the wilderness, and fought the world's greatest power for independence. Such people "did not mean," said Faulkner, "just to chase happiness, but to work for it." And by happiness they meant "not just pleasure, idleness, but peace, dignity, independence, and self-respect; that man's inalienable right was, the peace and freedom in which, by his own efforts and sweat, he could gain dignity and independence, owing nothing to any man."

Our forefathers knew what liberty was, because they were asserting it in a world in which most of mankind had long been without it: "We knew it once, had it once . . . Only something happened to us." We no longer "believed in liberty and freedom and independence, as the old fathers in the old strong, dangerous times had meant it."

In Faulkner's created world, happiness is never material. The pursuit of wealth and status again and again leads to a warped life—as with Jason Compson in *The Sound and the Fury* and Thomas Sutpen in *Absalom, Absalom,* and most vividly in the case of the soulless excuse for a human being Flem Snopes, who may be taken as a highlighted characterization of a certain type of American. Then there is the farmer whose world is shattered when he is told that the government will pay him *not* to grow cotton!

Whether he fully realized it or not, Faulkner in his world-class art and in his opinions was drawing from the well of traditional

Southern impulses. He even calls down the old truth that the price of liberty is eternal vigilance, that liberty is not a gift but only for those who have the character to get and keep it, "Which is exactly what we did, in those old days." John Taylor of Caroline, John C. Calhoun, and Robert E. Lee would know at once exactly what he meant. William Faulkner was not only a conservative Southerner, he believed that it was not such a bad thing to be.

Sam Ervin:
The Last Constitutionalist

In 1973, Senator Sam Ervin of North Carolina was perhaps the most respected and popular member of the United States Congress. His role in the televised Watergate hearings as chairman of the Senate Select Committee led one member of Congress to remark that he was "the most nonpartisan Democrat in the Senate." T-shirts were made in his honor; everyone had a favorite "Senator Sam" story; he starred on an album entitled "Senator Sam at Home;" his face was pressed on *Newsweek* and *Time*; fan clubs appeared; and it became "chic" to have a Southern accent and spin down-home tales of life in the rural South. Millions adored him. But Ervin didn't buy into this heroic public image. He was seventy-seven and had already decided he would retire in 1975. He maintained a listed phone number at his residence in Washington, D.C., for most of his time in the Senate (he only changed it after several unusual phone calls during the Watergate hearings led his wife to demand a new unlisted number), and he called himself a simple "country lawyer." He lived in the same house in Morganton, North Carolina, most of his life (across the street from his birth home), greeted neighbors and constituents himself at the front door, and graciously accepted produce on his porch from local farmers. He would often remark that his wife of more than fifty years kept him grounded. Senator Sam was truly one of the people.

Yet, Ervin's disarming smile, humorous stories, and folksy persona masked the depth of his intellect. This "country lawyer" took some of the most famous members of the Washington establishment to task for their flagrant violations of the Constitution. His autobiography, titled *Preserving the Constitution*, is a testament to the defining cause of his career, saving the Constitution of the Founders from the designs of "legislative and judicial activists . . . bent on remaking America in the image of their own thinking." He was rarely successful, but Ervin had a unique perspective on his many defeats. He believed Southerners had a:

certain peculiarity due to the fact that all of their greatest heroes were men who failed . . . men like Robert E. Lee, Stonewall Jackson and J. E. B. Stewart and those who followed them. These men failed in their objective, and the fact that they failed in their objective I think teaches some of us that the truth that's embodied in the little poem by Edwin Markham. . . . *Defeat may serve as well as victory to shake the soul and let the glory out,* and I think we need more of that spirit in this country that success is not the important thing, it's what you do and how you try to win success. . . . If you do not win success and you fight for your cause with valor, the defeat which you may suffer will shake the soul and let the glory out as well as victory will.

With such a colorful and important past, why has Ervin been forgotten? After scolding Richard Nixon for his abuse of executive powers during the Watergate hearings, Ervin was the darling of the progressive Left in 1973. At the same time, the finicky (and uninformed) Left often derided his supposed "inconsistency" with their worldview. The same Sam Ervin who relentlessly sought to check executive abuse in 1973 had stared down then-United States Attorney General and Leftist hero Robert F. Kennedy during congressional hearings on civil rights legislation, had opposed the Voting Rights Act of 1965 and the Civil Rights Act of 1964, and called Kennedy and other Northern men like him bigots for their apparent anti-Southern bias. How could such a constitutional scholar, they thought, support what were to them such unconstitutional positions?

It is the label "inconsistency" that has survived and that has descended Ervin into the depths of obscurity. He has been described as the intellectual mastermind of the "soft" Southern approach to blocking civil rights legislation. Under this charge, defending the Constitution was little more than a code-word for racism and "hate speech." Even his most recent biographer, Karl Campbell, claimed that Ervin's "preoccupation with maintaining the racial status quo contributed to an overly limited view of government power." According to Campbell, Ervin, in typical Southern fashion, favored the Constitution in the same way that Southern slaveholders clung to "virulent federalism" at the "Constitutional Convention in 1787" in order to protect "black chattel slavery, just as the strict constructionism and states' rights rhetoric of later generations of southerners served the cause of white supremacy." Campbell called this a "critical flaw in Ervin's constitutional philosophy." While Campbell applauded Ervin's approach to civil liberties and executive power, he also argued Ervin should have recognized that strong central authority is "sometimes necessary."

Not only is Campbell's characterization of Southern federalism in the early republic wrong, but his assessment of Ervin's cogency in defending the Constitution as some deep-seeded hatred for black Americans belies reality. If Ervin had simply used the Constitution to his advantage during the civil rights era and thrown it aside after that time, then Campbell and other critics of Ervin's public career would be correct; he would have been inconsistent. But Ervin's record is clear. He consistently and faithfully adhered to his oath to "support and defend the Constitution of the United States." Whether he was waging war against Richard Nixon, defending civil liberties in the 1960s, or pointing out the legal and constitutional flaws of civil rights legislation, Ervin was attempting to save the Constitution of the Founders. The struggle to preserve the Constitution was a struggle to uphold the founding principles of the United States. He was a Jeffersonian, a '76er, a states' rights Whig well versed in the American political tradition of decentralization. That is his legacy.

Sam J. Ervin, Jr., was born in Morganton, North Carolina, in 1896 as one of ten children to Sam J. Ervin, Sr., a well-respected trial lawyer in and around Burke County, and Laura Powe Ervin. Both the Ervins and Powes counted a number of ancestors who fought for American Independence and several members of both families, including Ervin's paternal grandfather, served in the Confederate army during the War Between the States. Sam Ervin, Sr., passed to his son a reverence for the Constitution as "the guardian of our liberties" and a disdain for "governmental tyranny and religious intolerance." He was reared on tales of Southern valor, and respected his father for carrying "his own sovereignty under his own hat," meaning "he adopted and advocated what he believed to be true, regardless of whether it coincided with views popularly held."

Ervin was also the consummate Southern gentleman and learned from his mother the values that molded his professional career: honesty, integrity, hard work, politeness, and most importantly, a reverence for tradition and place. He once wrote that he was:

> born of Burke County's bone and flesh of Burke County's flesh. Hence, outsiders may think I am biased in its favor. Be that as it may, I am satisfied that when the Good Lord restores the Garden of Eden to earth, He will center it in Burke County because He will have so few changes to make to achieve perfect creation.

Ervin enrolled at the University of North Carolina in 1913 and was graduated in 1917 while serving in Europe during World War I. The classical education he received influenced his love of literature and respect for history. Ervin counted the history professors at North Carolina as his greatest influences. History, they taught him, "is the torch of truth, and as such is forever illuminated across the centuries the laws of right and wrong," and from J. G. de Roulhac Hamilton, the dean of North Carolina history, Ervin learned that "one cannot understand the institutions of today unless he understands the events of yesterday which brought them into being." Of particular and lasting importance was a speech given by University President Edward Kidder Graham during chapel hour one morning where he insisted that the young men remember that the Magna Charta, the English Petition of Right, the English Bill of Rights, the Declaration of Independence, and the United States Constitution were "the great documents of history. These are living documents. Cut them, and they will bleed with the blood of those who fashioned them and those who have nurtured them through the succeeding generations."

Ervin left the University of North Carolina and was commissioned a second lieutenant in the United States Army in 1917. He was part of the first expeditionary forces to land in France and participated in the Battle of Soissons. He was wounded twice (once at Cantigny before Soissons) and awarded the Distinguished Service Cross for his leadership in capturing a German machine-gun nest during the action at Soissons. He was honorably discharged in 1919 and returned to Morganton to practice law. Most in North Carolina did not know that Ervin had been reduced to the rank of private early in the war for abandoning his command. This was only revealed in his autobiography shortly before his death in 1985. Regardless, Ervin bore the scars of Soissons for the rest of his life and his gallant actions saved the lives of many men. Shortly before the battle of Soissons, Ervin recounted that the company chaplain, a Catholic Priest, had said, "Before tomorrow's sun sets, many of you I see standing before me in the vigor of youth will have made the supreme sacrifice on the battlefield for the America all of us love." Ervin never forgot those words, and whether it was at Soissons, North Carolina, or Washington, D.C., he continued to fight for the America he loved and the founding principles of the United States for the remainder of his life.

After returning to Morganton, Ervin was admitted to the North Carolina Bar in 1919 and enrolled in Harvard Law School the same year. He was the only person in the history of the school to complete his work in reverse order, taking the third year classes first, then the second, until he finished his final examinations in 1922. He practiced law at his family firm, Ervin and Ervin, until 1937, and served in a number of elected positions in North Carolina, most importantly as a member of the North Carolina General Assembly in 1923, 1925, and 1931. While in the state legislature, Ervin displayed the same principled defense of civil liberty that would mark his career in the United States Senate. He opposed attempts to prohibit the instruction of evolution in North Carolina public schools—Ervin considered freedom of religion the most essential liberty—and fought for increased funding for black schools in Morganton and elsewhere. He was appointed Special Superior Court Judge in 1937 and held that appointment until 1943.

He was elected to the United States House of Representatives in 1946 and served for one year. This introduced Ervin to federal politics, but he was happy in North Carolina and declined to seek reelection. Yet, his time in the House impressed upon him that "the framers of the Constitution of the United States and North Carolina gave us a government of laws rather than a government of men. Fidelity to the government of laws is essential if good government, the reign of law, and liberty are to endure in our land." He was appointed to the North Carolina Supreme Court in 1948 and served until 1954, when he was sent to the United States Senate. Ervin summed up his career in the North Carolina Supreme Court in one of his opinions: "Ministers of the law ought not to permit zeal for its enforcement to cause them to transgress its precepts. They should remember that where law ends, tyranny begins." This bit of legal philosophy exemplified his political career in Washington and would make him at one time the most famous man in Congress.

Ervin was a statesman, a man who stood on principles rather than the ebb and flow of popular opinion. He was regarded as an independent Democrat and often voted with Republicans when he believed "that their position right." No one could corral him, and he infuriated opponents by refusing to acknowledge their attacks. This made him popular and powerful in Washington. He believed in the traditional role of a United States Senator, meaning he represented the people of the *State* of North Carolina in Washington, rather than the amorphous mass of the American people. "The Founding Fathers," he said, "accepted as verity this aphorism of the English Philosopher Thomas Hobbes: 'Freedom is political power divided into small fragments.'" As a consequence, Ervin argued that the states and local government were an essential component of the American political system:

> Local process of law are an essential part of good government because the national government cannot be as closely in contact with those who are governed as can the local authorities in the States and their several subdivisions. Local government is the only breakwater against the ever-pounding surf of the national government's demand for conformity to its delegates, a demand that threatens to submerge the individual and destroy the only kind of society in which personality can exist.

His indictment of the centralization of power in Washington spared no one. He contended judicial activism on the part of the Supreme Court "expanded the powers of the federal government and their own powers and diminished the powers of the States." Centralization made it possible for corrupt lobbyists to force congress to do their bidding, for it was "easier and more productive to deal with one legislative body, Congress, then to deal with 50 state legislatures." The executive branch "usurped the power of Congress to legislate by executive orders, and Congress sometimes abdicated its power to legislate to the Presidency by enacting vague statutes that delegated to the enforcing department or agency the authority to make implementing regulations." The end result was the destruction of "good government . . . the freedom of individuals [and] fiscal sanity."

Corruption was one of the primary fears of the Jeffersonians, and it was why they preferred diffusion of power. Ervin lamented that the corruption in Washington during his time was "aided and abetted by the public officials of many of the States who accepted dictation from federal departments and agencies in return for grants and loans of federal moneys." The end result was debt and fiscal irresponsibility. "Congress spurned both honest and intelligent choices . . . until it overwhelmed our nation with ruinous inflation and the most enormous national debt of any nation on earth." Ervin contended that excessive spending was "dishonest because it creates inflation, and inflation robs the past of its savings, the present of its economic power, and the future of its hopes as well as its unearned income." And fiscal irresponsibility did not stop at American borders. To Ervin, the United States had become:

> an international Santa Claus, who scatters untold billions of dollars of the patrimony of our people among multitudes of foreign nations, some needy and some otherwise, in the pious hope that America can thereby purchase friends and peace in the international world, and induce some foreign nations to reform their internal affairs in ways pleasing to the dispensers of our largess.

This was Hamiltonianism run amok. Patronage and dollars were, and still are, used to buy votes and centralize authority. This made Ervin's independency refreshing.

There were two issues that defined Sam Ervin's senatorial career: his opposition to federal civil rights legislation and his political war with Richard Nixon. In both cases, Ervin displayed a principled defense of the Constitution and the "federated Republic" of the Founders. His opposition to the Civil Rights movement has become a thorny issue in recent years and has made Ervin, along with other members of the "Southern bloc" of the United States Senate, pariahs in American history. They have been characterized as race baiters, thugs, and old-fashioned advocates of a social order contradictory to the founding principles of the United States. In regard to men like Theodore Bilbo of Mississippi, the first two descriptions are true—Ervin distanced himself from such rhetoric—but Ervin took issue with the last statement, not out of racial hatred, but because he argued civil rights legislation *destroyed* the Union of the Founders. His positions were Jeffersonian and displayed a legal brilliance virtually unsurpassed by modern constitutional scholars.

Biographer Karl Campbell called Ervin's tactics "insidious." This is more a reflection on Campbell's biases than Ervin's constitutional philosophy. Ervin publically insisted he harbored no ill will toward black Americans. He had, in fact, championed better treatment for North Carolina's black population on several occasions while serving as a member of the North Carolina legislature, and nary a private statement could be found linking him to the racist rhetoric that is often attached to opponents of civil rights. Biographer Paul Clancy summed up his opposition this way:

> Ervin fought civil rights legislation, in part, because he had to. . . . He saw the need for correcting the injustice of job discrimination, ghetto housing, and segregated schools. But passing federal legislation, setting up a federal bureaucracy to administer it, and aiming it—especially aiming it—at the South put Ervin in a corner. Like Robert E. Lee, who did not agree with everything that was going on in the South, Ervin felt it was his duty to fight. Like Lee, Ervin believed that "duty" was the most sublime word in the language.

Ervin anticipated the type of attacks that would be used against him both during and after his time in Congress. The most common was the claim of inconsistency, a charge that virtually every article or book written about Ervin contains. In his autobiography, he succinctly defended his work against civil rights legislation in the hope of disarming these attacks:

> Many persons of undoubted sincerity deem all civil rights proposals as sacrosanct and all persons who oppose them to be racial bigots. They charge me with inconsistency in advocating equal civil liberties for all Americans and opposing special civil rights for Americans of minority races. My positions in these respects are not inconsistent. They are completely harmonious. Equal civil liberties for all and special civil rights for some are incompatible in concept and in operation. . . . There is an unbridgeable gap between civil liberties and civil rights. Civil liberties belong to Americans of all races, classes, and conditions. Civil rights are special privileges enacted by Congress, or created by executive regulations, or manufactured by activist Supreme Court Justices for the supposed benefit of members of minority races on the basis of their race.

What many Americans viewed as moral justice Ervin saw as an affront to constitutional government and a slippery slope to tyranny and the destruction of the Union of the Founders. As a member of the Senate Judiciary Subcommittee on Constitutional Rights, Ervin was in the unique position to filet any civil rights bill that came before the Senate. Between 1957 and 1972, there were dozens. Ervin labeled each one "unconstitutional . . . tyrannical, or unnecessary," and while he could not kill most, he succeeded in watering down or delaying most of them. In every case, the Constitution was his shield and history his sword.

Ervin first went on the offensive in 1957. President Dwight Eisenhower insisted on a civil rights legislation package and put pressure on Congress to act. Ervin called the proposed 1957 civil rights act "utterly repugnant to the American constitutional and legal systems." In a long indictment of the bill, Ervin explained that the American tradition was built on legal safeguards and that the founding generation, both during the American War for Independence and afterward, steadfastly determined to ensure that Americans would never face the same type of tyrannical government they suffered under in the 1760s and 1770s. In Ervin's mind, the most egregious affront to civil liberty was the denial of trial by jury. The 1957 civil rights bill removed that essential protection from the American people. As he noted in his autobiography:

> They [the Founders] knew that tranquility was not to be always anticipated in a republic; that strife would rise between classes and sections, and even civil war might come; and that in such time judges themselves might not be safely trusted in criminal cases, especially in prosecutions for political offenses, where the whole power of the executive is arrayed against the accused party. They knew that what was done in the past might be attempted in the future, and that troublous times would arise, when rulers and people would become restive under restraint, and seek by sharp and decisive methods to accomplish ends deemed just and proper and that the principles of constitutional liberty would be in peril, unless established by irrepealable law.

Ultimately, Ervin contended that every civil rights bill that crossed his desk violated the principles of American government, be it the Civil Rights Act of 1964, the Voting Rights Act of 1965, or the Equal Employment Opportunities Act of 1972. By creating federal departments and agencies with the power to act as "law-maker, prosecutor, jury, and judge in the same office or agency," these laws destroyed the separation of legislative, executive, and judicial powers the Founders considered essential to good government. Not only were these regulatory agencies unconstitutional, they were "inimical to due process, and fair play." And with the Supreme Court acting in concert with the legislative branch in declaring these laws constitutional, Ervin believed there was no hope for liberty or free government in America. In 1963, Ervin wrote:

> The proponents of current civil rights legislation, many of them undoubted men of good will, would, in an attempt to meet a genuine problem concerning the inflamed nature between the races in this

country, trounce upon an even more pressing need—the need to preserve limited, constitutional government in an age of mass bureaucracy and centralization.

Late in life, Ervin lamented that:

> The most serious threat to good government and freedom in America is not posed by evil-minded men and women. It is posed by legislative and judicial activists and other sincere persons of the best intentions, who are bent on remaking America in the image of their own thinking. They lack faith in the capacity of the people to be the masters of their own fates, and the captains of their own souls, and insist that government assume the task of controlling their thoughts and managing their lives.

Many Americans, particularly Northerners, considered Ervin a paranoid, delusional, bigoted, lunatic in the early 1960s, but by the Richard Nixon administration, many of his dire prophesies had come true, and it was Ervin, not the champions of unbridled central authority, who was proven correct.

Ervin believed executive abuse had been a problem since he first arrived in the United States Senate. He had battled with the Eisenhower administration—Eisenhower in fact coined the term "executive privilege"—over withholding information from the Congress. Every occupant of the White House from that point forward expanded on the fabricated "privilege," but Richard Nixon used the tactic better than anyone before him. Ervin feared the effect Nixon was having on free government. His administration was infamous for invoking "executive privilege" to enhance the power of the executive, mostly at the expense of Congress and the states. Ervin lamented Congress was partly responsible for the problem. "In all candor, we in the legislative branch must confess that the shifting of power to the executive has resulted from our failure to assert our constitutional powers." The end result in his mind would be "a government of men, not of laws." Here again was the corruption that Ervin dreaded.

Nixon was not the first to appoint "czars" to circumvent the legislative process and arrogate power to the executive, but to that time he was perhaps the most flagrant in their use. Additionally, Nixon supported trouncing civil liberties in the name of "national security" and withheld critical information on the Vietnam War under the guise of "executive privilege." At every turn, Ervin attempted to block this spiraling trend toward centralization. Though reluctant to serve as chairman of the Watergate hearings, Ervin eventually viewed this role as the opportunity to expose the "imperial presidency" and crush usurpation of power by the executive branch. He admitted that finding the truth in the Watergate conspiracy represented a "herculean task," but he was up for the challenge and viewed it as his duty to act.

In his opening statement during the Watergate hearings, Ervin said:

> The Founding Fathers, having participated in the struggle against arbitrary power, comprehended some eternal truths respecting men and government. They knew that those who are entrusted with power are susceptible to the disease of tyrants which George Washington rightly described as "love of power and the proneness to abuse it." For that reason, they realized that the power of public officers should be defined by laws which they, as well as the people, are obligated to obey.

His Jeffersonian view of executive authority led him to conclude, "In my judgment the President's power under the Constitution in respect to all congressional acts of which he disapproves is limited to vetoing them, and allowing Congress to nullify his veto by a two-thirds majority in each House if it so desires." As he said more succinctly, "Divine right went out with the American Revolution."

Through Ervin's crafty use of wit, humor, charm, and a penchant for knowing what to say and when to say it, it became clear to the American public that Nixon, and essentially every American president, had become an elected king. Ervin had finally removed the shroud of deception, something he had been attempting to do for almost twenty years. It was bittersweet justice. Nixon buckled and later resigned due in large part to Ervin's brilliant performance during the Watergate investigations, but by the late seventies it seemed that Americans forgot or failed to heed the lessons of 1973.

Nixon's enforcers tried to tarnish both Ervin and the committee hearings by labeling them as pure partisanship and a witch hunt to destroy a Republican president. To Ervin they were not—he was searching for "truth and honor"—but to many Democrats, the label stuck. As long as "their guy" was in office, Democrats cared little for executive restraint, civil liberties, or the Constitution. Republicans were no different. Ervin, however, was a dying breed of American statesman, one that has rarely darkened the halls of Congress in the modern era. He would vote his conscience, even if it meant he was the lone voice of opposition, as he sometimes was. Ervin proudly held up his congressional voting record as a model of consistency. When he retired in January 1975, everyone recognized Senator Sam as the most principled man in Congress, if not Washington, D.C. There has been no-one like him since.

Biographer Karl Campbell labeled him a conservative obstructionist bent on preserving the "southern status quo," most importantly the "racism, civility, and paternalism" of the South. To men like Campbell, there has to be a deeper, more sinister motivation to states' rights, strict construction, or a principled defense of republicanism than simply "defending the Constitution."

Certainly, culture shapes many decisions in life, and Burke County was in Ervin's blood and bones, but to suggest that the Constitution was nothing more than a utilitarian means of enforcing Ervin's world-view, as Campbell does, is to sell short Ervin and his principled defense of American conservatism. Ervin considered the Constitution sacrosanct, because he considered the American tradition and the principles of '76 sacrosanct. As Ervin said in an interview with William F. Buckley in 1978, "I think that if you have to violate your constitution in order to save your country—you have to lose your constitution—I think your country's lost anyway." It had been lost since 1861, but at least with men like Ervin around, a little bit of the spirit of '76 remained in the federal capital. Not only was Ervin the last constitutionalist, he was the last Democrat in the Jeffersonian tradition.

M. E. Bradford and the American Founding

The most important year in the modern conservative movement, if such a thing exists, is 1981. Most would point to Ronald Reagan's inauguration, but while that event was significant, it was a little-known controversy over a potential political appointment that changed the intellectual underpinnings of "conservatism" in the United States. The year 1981 split the way Americans think about their past. This was nothing new. There have been at various times in the American "conservative movement" differences in vision, theory, and direction. The most famous have tended to be over foreign policy. Most believe that problems such as taxes, the size and scope of government, and other "domestic" concerns are common ground for conservatives—if it were only that simple.

Since the late 1970s, there has been an intellectual war in the conservative movement on the meaning of American history and the founding period in particular. The scholar M. E. Bradford was at the center of the storm. He was nominated by president-elect Reagan in 1980 for the chair of the National Endowment for the Humanities and had the support of several prominent conservatives, including Russell Kirk, Forrest McDonald, and Eugene Genovese. This was a tremendous honor and ultimately an important post. Bradford would have been able to use the resources of the federal government to advance his interpretation of the founding period and American history. But as a Southerner with views that ran contrary to the "accepted" narrative—most importantly his steadfast disdain for Abraham Lincoln—his appointment was not going to be easy.

Almost immediately, Bradford's opponents such as Norman Podhoretz and Irving and William Kristol went on the offensive. Unable to challenge Bradford's positions intellectually, they dredged up Bradford's support for George Wallace in 1972 as proof that he was, in fact, a racist! Podhoretz and the Kristols used the *New York Times* to advance their agenda and Reagan, feeling the political pressure, withdrew Bradford from consideration and instead nominated William Bennett in 1981, a proud proponent of, in his own words, "neo-conservatism." Bradford and his supporters, now classified as "paleo-conservatives" in contrast to the "neo-conservatives" like Bennett, Podhoretz, and the Kristols, never forgave either Reagan or the Republican establishment and splintered the "Reagan Revolution." The political impact was minimal, but the intellectual and theoretical results have had a lasting effect on the way Americans regard the founding. If Bradford had been appointed, the Founding Fathers and the Constitution may be viewed differently today.

Bradford was born in Texas in 1934. He attended the University of Oklahoma and received a PhD in literature from Vanderbilt University where he studied under the Southern agrarian Donald Davidson. His academic training at Vanderbilt was unsurpassed. Bradford was the model "interdisciplinary" scholar before that word became chic. He was a professor of English and later taught political philosophy at the University of Dallas. Bradford peppered his writings on American history with references to literature, philosophy, classical history, and theology. He was an accomplished scholar on William Faulkner, and in addition to several works on the Southern agrarians, such as Andrew Lytle and Allen Tate, he helped revitalize a latent interest in Southern literature as editor of the *Southern Classics Series*. It was said that Bradford could take four hours to write a paragraph. He would read, digest, and then draw on his considerable intellectual resources to make a point, often in a way that most writers cannot do. That was the beauty of Mel Bradford. His words had to be chewed.

Bradford produced three important works on the founding: *A Better Guide Than Reason* (1979); *A Worthy Company,* later renamed *Founding Fathers,* (1988); and *Original Intentions* (1993). His *Against the Barbarians* (1992) also contained several chapters on members of the founding generation. A unifying theme of each is the conservative nature of the American founding. Bradford argued a respect and establishment for the rule of law, real property, and the ritual of the mundane made Americans resistant to the Jacobinism of the French Revolution. Americans, he said, were republicans before the Republic existed. The Declaration of Independence and the Constitution did not make Americans; Americans and the American experience made them. And though Bradford did not call the War for Independence a conservative event, its effects, he said, were nevertheless conservative. This is what separated Bradford from other scholars of the founding period, such as Louis Hartz, Gordon Wood, and Harry Jaffa. In Bradford's analysis, their version of the American founding, as a radical departure from accepted norms, morals, and customs, does not fit with the history of the period. Bradford forcefully contended Americans were a conservative lot looking to preserve the ancient traditions of their past, nothing more. To view it any other way would be a distortion of the founding generation and their original intent.

Bradford's *A Better Guide Than Reason* ranks among the top conservative tomes in American history and should be coupled with Russell Kirk's seminal *Conservative Mind* as mandatory reading for American conservatives. The work is a sweeping refutation of the liberal and Leftist view of American history from the founding period through the War Between the States. Each chapter is a significant contribution to a conservative view of the past, from his opening piece on the influence of classical scholarship on the founding generation, to his concluding chapter on Kirk's "moral patrimony." And each is a first-rate historical and philosophical treatise that should be reviewed and absorbed independently.

As Bradford wrote in "A Teaching For Republicans: Roman History and the Nation's First Identity,"

> What our fathers called Washington City is thus, at one and the same time, a symbol of their common political aspirations and a specification of the continuity of those objectives with what they knew of the Roman experience. . . . For gentlemen of the eighteen century, Rome was the obvious point of reference when the conversation turned to republican theory.

This origination point is important, for if the founding generation were grounded in principles that predated the American experience, and if they were guided by something greater than a newly formed respect for "natural rights," then the American tradition was something older and stouter than eighteenth-century liberalism and the founding documents were an American adaptation of centuries of experience rather than an "American creation" as Joseph Ellis called it. The roots of the American federal republic stretched to the Tiber River.

Bradford argued that all men in the founding generation felt a conscious connection to Rome. In the process, they built "a modified Whig Rome" in America. Most importantly,

> our first Americans did not see in independence a sharp departure from the identity they already enjoyed. Rather, both of these developments were, above all else, necessities for the protection of an already established society: necessities like those behind Rome's own republican development. . . . Even in whatever they attempted that seemed new.

Bradford insisted (correctly) that "American Whiggery is (or was) closer to that of Edmund Burke than to the nostrums of Priestley and Fox. And is no relation whatsoever to the 'virtue' preached by Robespierre." Rather than a fundamental shift in the societal order like the French Revolution, the American War for Independence *preserved* the ancient identities of the West.

He took this theme further in his "The Heresy of Equality: A Reply to Harry Jaffa." He began the essay with a definitive conservative statement:

> Equality as a moral or political imperative . . . is the antonym of every legitimate conservative principle. Contrary to most Liberals, new and old, it is nothing less than sophistry to distinguish between equality of opportunity . . . and equality of condition. . . . For only those who *are* equal can take equal advantage of a given circumstance. And there is no man equal to any other, except perhaps in the special, and politically untranslatable, understanding of the Deity. *Not intellectually or physically or economically or even morally. Not equal!* Such is, of course, the genuinely self-evident proposition.

Bradford wrote this to differentiate his position on the American founding from Harry Jaffa's. Jaffa argued that Jefferson's "all men are created equal" formed the bedrock of the American political tradition. To Jaffa, this was new, radical, and fundamentally different from the established structure the founding generation enjoyed as British subjects. American conservatism, in essence, was *created* in 1776.

Bradford pointed out that while Jaffa may call himself a conservative and his position conservative, "his conservatism is of a relatively recent variety and is, in substance, Old Liberalism hidden under a Union battle flag." It was impossible, in Bradford's mind, to assume that American conservatism can be divorced from the "funded wisdom of the ages." He wrote, "only a relativist or historicist could argue that American conservatism should be an utterly unique phenomenon, without antecedents which predate 1776 and unconnected with the mainstream of English and European thought and practice known to our forefathers in colonial times." This was more than a battle over the founding tradition; it was a war to determine the intellectual underpinnings of American conservatism.

The Declaration of Independence was at the heart of the contest. Jaffa's Declaration created new rights, new philosophies, and a new order: an American exceptionalism that Americans from 1776 forward, including Abraham Lincoln and the Union army, fought to preserve. Bradford called this a historical distortion:

> To anyone familiar with English letters and the English mind in the seventeenth and eighteenth centuries, the Declaration of Independence is clearly a document produced out of the *mores majorum*—legal, rhetorical, poetic—and not a piece of reasoning or systematic truth. No sentence of its whole means anything out of context. It unfolds *seriatim* and makes sense only when read through. Furthermore, what it does mean is intelligible only in a matrix of circumstances—political, literary, linguistic, and mundane.

If Jaffa was correct, then the American experience was one of reform, not the kind that enhances the existing order, but the sweeping, radical, wholesale type of reform pursued by fire and sword and promulgated by the Left. Bradford contended this was, and is, neoconservatism—not the American order—an order that was older and fundamentally conservative in the Roman and British Whig mold. "Said another way, the more people derive their political identity from Lincoln's [and by default Jaffa's] version of Equality, the more they are going to push against the given and providential frame of things to prove up the magic phrase."

Bradford concluded *A Better Guide Than Reason* with a review of Russell Kirk's *The Roots of American Order*. The two men fundamentally agree on every issue concerning the American founding and the historical precedents that made America. Kirk, Bradford stated:

> contends our roots run deep and remain intact, that to know them is to recognize both their antiquity and their present hold upon us. His book is a calculated inquiry into the genesis of our national

character which looks behind events and documents to remote antecedents and attempts to encourage a modest estimation of its originality, a thoughtful appreciation of how much and how far it was brought to these shores, and a quiet rejoicing that we remain, in our essential qualities as a people, so well and so anciently grounded in the funded wisdom of the ages.

That was the driving theme of Bradford's work as well. Moreover, he was inspired by Kirk to continue the process:

Let us have narratives, mixed with generous portions of biography and analogue, and a quiet emphasis on commitments shaping the actions of those involved long before they have found theoretical expression. Let us demonstrate how the bonds of faith, friendship, family, and common experience have ordinarily obtained in our national affairs, whatever abstract explanations are imposed them after the fact.

Bradford took his own advice and produced one of the best but forgotten works on the founding generation.

Bradford was not a novice in biography when he wrote *Founding Fathers* in 1981. He had expounded on several members of the founding generation in his *A Better Guide Than Reason* and his essays always included biographical sketches designed to anchor the subject in time and place. People were not abstract and therefore events and thoughts could not happen in the abstract. They were complex, and Bradford always made a point to highlight those complexities. As biography drove Kirk's *Conservative Mind,* so biography drove Bradford's works, and his *Founding Fathers* was, in essence, the culmination of his academic and philosophical interest in the American conservative tradition. Outside of those on the Right and typically those who are considered Old Right, the book is generally ignored, but it should not be. Its fifty-five "pocket" biographies of the men who drafted the Constitution are a sweeping narrative of the culture, ideas, and principles that contributed to the American order.

Bradford had his favorites. He had already written fine sketches on John Dickinson and Patrick Henry, and though Henry was not included in *Founding Fathers,* his spirit and devotion to the "lamp of experience" is readily evident. Bradford, of course, used Dickinson's words as the title of *A Better Guide Than Reason,* and to Bradford, it was Dickinson and men of his stripe who saved the

1787 Philadelphia Convention from the designs of scheming men, notably James Wilson, James Madison, Alexander Hamilton, and Gouverneur Morris.

Bradford called Dickinson "the most undervalued and misunderstood member of their notable company." He was the "American Burke, the faithful steward of an old regime." He championed "the American version of the ancient patterns of English life and law that produced stability in the mother country." In many respects, Bradford argued the Constitution was *his* Constitution, at least in the way it was explained in the state ratifying conventions. He was the sober balance between those who could see the need for a stronger central authority and those who understood that centralization could lead to absolute tyranny. Yet, Dickinson was not alone in this regard. Men such as Roger Sherman of Connecticut, William Richardson Davie and Hugh Williamson of North Carolina, and John Rutledge of South Carolina shared this same type of conservatism. These men, not James Madison, were the "Fathers of the Constitution" in Bradford's mind. They are what made the Constitution a conservative document in the ancient tradition.

He described all of the delegates to the Philadelphia Convention as "men of the eighteenth century, but of the English and Scottish Enlightenment, not the French." This dichotomy was important, for the English Enlightenment was planted more firmly in the ancient order than the French, and it must be remembered that the French philosophers were the driving intellectual force behind the radical French Revolution, a type of Revolution not seen on American soil. Bradford also contended that the majority of the delegates had more in common than not. They were well educated, mostly Christians, who believed in a "federal system of checks and balances under a sovereign law." But that sovereign law had limits, for "they were careful to limit the fundamental scope of the law itself, leaving what they called 'internal police' and many of the great questions concerning value and faith to the regulation of state and local governments and to the operation of society itself." In other words, the Founding Fathers believed in decentralized, local government, often called in the modern era "states' rights."

What Bradford did in *Founding Fathers* was unique. His collection of snapshots into the lives of the framers of the Constitution grounded the document in the cultural, political, and social realities of the early American republic. Biographies on many of the men had been written before, but no one had gathered them together in a way that showcased their overarching similarities and resolve to *preserve* the old order (and not in regard to slavery as most leftist histories of the event conclude). Historians more often noted the Founders for their differences than similarities. But in Bradford's analysis, perhaps only six and no more than ten of the delegates favored a design of government radically different from the Articles of Confederation. There was more consensus than conflict. That should be the lesson of the Philadelphia Convention, and though the Constitution was not given its final form until the State Ratifying Conventions had their say, Bradford showed that the "anti-Federalist" spirit and critique of the document (limited centralization and states' rights) was not born after it was written.

Founding Fathers led to *Original Intentions*. Written in honor of the bicentennial in 1987, it is a sweeping eight-chapter text that addressed both the Philadelphia Convention and the State Ratifying Conventions. Bradford's conclusion from *Founding Fathers* remained unchanged. "Concerning the Framers, these essays have ... demonstrated that, despite their many other differences, limited government (as opposed to anarchic freedom) was uniformly their objective." This is a book dominated by the conservative voices of what Russell Kirk called prescription. The men who wrote and ratified the Constitution and who had the greatest role in its formation were not influenced by rational speculation. They were products of an age and a tradition and their wisdom led to a document different from what James Madison proposed in the early days of the Philadelphia Convention. Bradford, in fact, called Madison's role in the Convention little more than a "comic action" and described him as more of an annoyance than a sage.

Bradford consistently referred to the actions of "wiser men" in the work of the Convention and the influence of history upon them. The British example of constitutional government weighed heavily upon the delegates to the Philadelphia Convention and those who ratified it in the states. It could not have happened otherwise. It was history that thwarted the Virginia Plan and Madison's attempts to crush the states in the opening debates in Philadelphia. It was history that led to the "anti-Federalist" response to the document when it reached the states for ratification. It was history that determined what type of

Republic the American people would accept. Bradford argued:

> It is impossible to understand what the Framers attempted with the Constitution of the United States without first recognizing why most of them dreaded pure democracy, judicial tyranny, or absolute legislative supremacy, and sought instead to secure for themselves and their posterity the sort of specific, negative, and procedural guarantees that have grown up within the context of that . . . most stable and continuous version of the rule of law known to the civilized word: the premise [fostered by the British system of government] that every free citizen should be protected by the law of the land.

Bradford expressed both optimism and pessimism in this work. He believed "the old Republic of the Fathers is still there, visible within the misshapen effulgence of the United States Constitution as we presently experience it, waiting to have the barnacles cleaned away that, as amended, it may once more shine forth among the nations." But, he doubted that he was winning his long battle against the distorted version of the early republic advanced by Jaffa and other of his persuasion. "The old confusion," he wrote, "between the Constitution and the language concerning equality in the Declaration of Independence persists, even now, almost unabated. Indeed, I might well ague that it grows to be more and more entrenched with each passing decade." He hoped that by writing *Original Intentions*, he could help Americans understand that the Constitution was not a theoretical statement of lofty principles, radical designs, or democratic centralization. Rather:

> the powers of the new government are few and explicit is . . . the central theme of the Federalist defense of the United States Constitution and a primary explanation of why the sequence of ratifications went as it did. If we would understand these results and the enthusiasm with which an essentially conservative people looked forward with hope to life under the new government that they made possible, then we should find ground for them in "minimalist" interpretations of the authority that was created.

Bradford's contributions to American history have been overshadowed by the "professional" class of historians in the academy. He did not belong, and in reality, could not belong with them. That is his badge of honor. He spent years trying to save the founding generation from the denizens of history departments across the country. They, for the most part, rejected him and have marginalized his work. Graduate students would be hard pressed to find a Mel Bradford treatise on the founding generation among their required reading lists. Bradford should have expected as much. His independence, however, is and was a refreshing statement of the American spirit, and he has left the American people, not just academics, with an inheritance and an intellectual legacy. Like the men to whom he dedicated his life writing about, his words are timeless.

Bradford wrote in *Remembering Who We Are* that:

> The American statesman, the good pilot, steers us back to a course well charted by those wise Fathers whose example is still available in the recorded glory of their times. To remember our origins—where we come from—is still a part of the answer as to where we should go. And it is for this reason we build libraries, that the living word should be preserved among us.

He was more than a philosopher or historian. Bradford was a statesman in the American tradition.

A Mass for the Resurrection: Who Owns America?

In graduate school, I was assigned by the resident "New South" historian *I'll Take My Stand* by Twelve Southerners as my final paper. I eagerly accepted the project. This was in my back-yard, so to speak. I had read the book at least twice before and considered it one of the best tomes on Southern culture and more accurately the American tradition. I received a "B+." After I presented my paper to the class, the professor explained that I was too sentimental. The authors were, in his mind, Utopian romantics who had never worked a farm and therefore could not understand how terrible the agrarian life had been for most Southerners. This liberal academic advocated an industrialized South, for in farming he could see only economic backwardness, poverty, and social decline. Industry saved the South from her sins and buried the ghosts of the past.

His critique was, unfortunately, typical. Since the work was published in 1930, most reactions to the subject material have been negative. The "Southern Agrarians" as they have been called were branded fascists, reactionaries, racists, and every other name a Reconstructed Southerner or self-righteous Yankee could throw at them. Agrarianism did not fit their American paradigm. I also remember the hippie Leftist fellow who sat next to me in class raving over the book. To him, it had an environmental appeal that most missed. He was right. *I'll Take My Stand* should have broad appeal to Americans. It is a treatise of independence, both economic and social: a study of the best elements of a prosperous society. It is Jeffersonian and uniquely American, not just Southern. As Donald Davidson wrote, "In its very backwardness the South had clung to some secret which embodied, it seemed, the elements out of which its own reconstruction—and possibly even the reconstruction of America—might be achieved." It is a song of hope.

Six years later, seven of the original twelve partnered with fourteen additional writers to produce *Who Owns America? A New Declaration of Independence*. This work disappeared from the American literary scene faster than *I'll Take My Stand*. It also received much of the same critique. Those on the American right—essentially the Hamiltonian strain which had long since destroyed their opponents—vigorously opposed its distaste for a capitalist economy. And, though the authors rejected capitalism, Marxists panned it because the book did not embrace their centralized prescription for societal change. Of course, none of the authors were Marxists, thankfully. Alan Tate explained that Marxists simply wanted to "keep capitalism with the capitalism left out." So what did these men and women want? If they rejected both capitalism and Marxism, what was left? To Americans who had been thoroughly reconstructed into the progressive industrialist order, these were the only choices that made sense.

Who Owns America? was written during the heart of the Great Depression, and most political and economic thinkers believed more centralization, not less, was needed to tame and then conquer the problem. It was evident around the world, from the rise of fascist, communist, and totalitarian governments in Europe, to the iron-fisted centralization of the New Deal and the Roosevelt administration, the West was having a love affair, it seemed, with supreme power. As the title states, *Who Owns America?* offered a different solution: political, economic, and social decentralization, a "new declaration of independence." That was the American tradition from the founding period forward and in 1936 it had only been recently destroyed. America, the real, tangible, beautiful America based on the republican ideals of small, independent, virtuous, politically engaged and astute farmers could be resurrected from the ashes, but drastic action needed to be taken. This was not romantic idealism. In contrast to the America reformers of all persuasions wanted, the America embodied in *Who Owns America?* was based on a real place time had forgotten. This was a conservative manifesto of the American variety.

As Frank Lawrence Owsley wrote in his essay "The Foundations of Democracy,"

> Neither Congress, President, nor Supreme Court knows at this moment what is the Constitution of the United States; and it can hardly be proved that the remaining one hundred and thirty million inhabitants of the United States possess any greater certainty about their Constitution than the three departments of the Federal Government which are sworn to uphold, maintain, and defend it.

We are, indeed, in a constitutional fog which has constantly grown thicker since the original document was presented to the country for ratification in 1787.

This is hardly a radical statement. Owsley, one of the original twelve agrarians, was pointing to the obvious in 1936. Americans had forgotten, or had purposely neglected, their distinctively American past.

Owsley placed the burden of this problem squarely on the backs of the Republican Party. They had maliciously transformed society by using the famed (or infamous) "higher law" doctrine of the 1850s:

> It was only after Lincoln's death that it became apparent that the "higher law" had been invoked, not to bring freedom and happiness to the slave, but rather to the great bankers, railroad magnates, and industrialists. . . . It short, it was in reality the industrialists and corporations who invoked the "higher law" to gain control of the National Government and make it over according to their desire.

Yet, Owsley emphasized that the "higher law" had been distorted. The Founders subscribed to a "higher law," just not the one advanced by the Republican Party from the 1850s onward. His "higher law," as expounded upon by Jefferson, Henry, Dickinson, and Samuel Adams, "*was and is the absolute denial of the totalitarian State; neither kings nor parliaments, foreign or domestic, had complete sovereignty over the individual.*"

This "higher law" was born from their common experience and history:

> from the Anglo-Saxon days when God was supposed to have made the laws and the king and his council only declared what they were; from the charter of Henry I, who acknowledged the supremacy of immemorial customs and laws; from King John, who signed the Magna Charta, and all the kings who came after him, who, in a similar fashion, admitted that their sovereignty over subjects was limited. The jurists Coke, Littleton, and Blackstone confirmed the limitations of sovereignty, and Browne, Hobbes, Milton, and Locke, the philosophers, stated in broad abstract terms the theories of limited sovereignty. The philosophers of the American Revolution stated these principles more clearly, and, as I have said, they made these principles the foundation of the American State. They were called "natural rights."

Included among the "natural rights," Owsley contended, was

the "right to self-government—that is government was made to serve man, man was not made to serve government, and when government failed to serve man it should be changed, peaceably if possible, forcibly if need be."

Owsley argued those who supported the original interpretation of "natural rights" and the "higher law" were the Jeffersonians. They defined American conservatism—a conservatism based on the "cardinal principle of self-government." And it was founded on their understanding of human history, most importantly their collective colonial experience:

> The knowledge gained from experience as English colonists demonstrated irrefutably to these men that government from a great distance, by legislators not equally affected by their laws with the people for whom they were legislating, was ignorant government because it had no understanding of the local situation; and it was despotic government because the opinion and wishes of the people for whom the laws were passed were not considered or even known.

The Jeffersonians utilized the commonly used terms "states' rights" and "strict construction," Owsley contended, as either "*aspects of the great principles of the right of self-government*" or as "*defensive weapons against what the Jeffersonians believed to be the enemies of the basic principles of the American State.*" Thus, both terms were born from practical American experience but were rooted in something tangible: history and human experience.

But Owsley also believed Jefferson and Samuel Adams would not support strict construction or states' rights today:

> They would, probably, according to their own logic, advocate *regional governments*; and realists as they were, they would hardly be able to look at the two hundred and ninety-odd volumes of Supreme Court decisions and remain strict constructionists. Without doubt they would demand a new Constitution which guaranteed unequivocally the basic principles of democracy.

Central to a democratic government was the wide distribution of property and the resulting independence of the American people. It was only by securing the traditional "natural rights" of the American founding that the United States and the American people would be able to protect against "the fascist or communist totalitarian State which guarantees security and denies freedom."

Donald Davidson, another of the original Twelve Southerners, carried the theme further in an essay titled "That This Nation May Endure—The Need for Political Regionalism." Davidson lamented that since the 1850s, Americans had looked upon regional differences, often classified as sectional differences, with disdain. They were more readily seen as a curse upon nationalism and the Union than a blessing, but Davidson flipped that notion on its head. In a purely Jeffersonian way of looking at the United States—Jefferson after all did believe that the North American continent would at one point contain several autonomous regional governments—Davidson stated that, "The diversity of regions rather enriches the national life than impoverishes it, and their mere existence as regions cannot be said to constitute a problem. Rather in their differences they are a national advantage, offering not only the charm of variety but he interplay of points of view that ought to give flexibility and wisdom."

Under the flag of "nation" the United States experienced several waves of regional imperialism facilitated by the Constitution, a document Davidson contends was ill equipped to handle regional or sectional differences. The central villain in the modern era had been the Northeast, a region which considered the South conquered provinces after the War Between the States, and that forced its political-economic vision—Hamiltonianism—on the rest of the United States by manipulating the powers of the central government. Every president from "Grant to Hoover," Davidson wrote, has "represented the will of the Northeast and fostered the welfare of the Northeast." The result was an unbalanced United States, the "towers of New York . . . built upon Southern and Western backs." Davidson considered the New Deal a frontal assault by a combination of the West and the South against the imperialist Northeast. But it, in kind, would only produce another round of regional imperialism against the Northeast. Although he thought some in the South and the West considered this retribution just, he was not among that group. He warned that Americans must recall "Burke's great saying about not drawing an indictment against a whole people, we should remember gallantries and beneficences as well as errors." In other words, there were always good, hard-working, honest, and just Northerners. Yankees could not be counted among them.

Regional governments, he surmised, would *save* rather than

imperil the Union, for the Union of the Founders had long since disappeared and had been replaced with a government destructive to the liberty, independence, and cultural uniqueness of the American people. How this would be accomplished was a matter of debate. Owsley, among others, had suggested a new constitution, and Davidson agreed that this method of reform was preferable to any other. Yet, he was skeptical, and rightly so, that this could be pulled off by modern American society:

> Whatever may be said of this bold and well-argued proposal, there is no doubt that it quickens our minds, as other schemes do not, with a sense of possible and statesmanlike achievement rather than dulls us with a cynical yielding to the grind of abstract force and blind accident. If the Constitution is to be rewritten, the drafting must be done by men who, like the fathers of the original Constitution, believe in the power of humanity over circumstance, and can bring to the task of constitution-making something more than the statistical and technical knowledge of the modern expert, and a great deal more than the sleek political knowledge which is the average American politician's substitute for statesmanship. The task requires men who are, as Madison and his colleagues were, at once lawyers, philosophers, students of history, men of letters, and men of the world, and who have the "feel" of the American situation as well as acquaintance with theory.

What Americans needed most was independence in the old sense, *i.e.*, the end of the neo-colonialism of the Northeast. Davidson supported any proposal short of totalitarianism, communism, or fascism that would bring about the restoration of "small business, well-distributed property and an agrarian regime . . . content with modest returns." In an argument that harkened back to the opponents of the Constitution (the true federalists) and John Taylor of Caroline, Davidson supported regional government because it was the most beneficial to the American people as a whole. It was truly *national.* "Among other things," Davidson said, "it means that the land and the region belong to the people who dwell there, and that they will be governed only by their own consent." That was American democracy and the American tradition guided by the lamp of experience.

Perhaps the most interesting essays of the book dealt with the social and cultural dislocation of modern America. Two are of note. The first, titled "The Emancipated Woman" by Mary Shattuck

Fisher, was a judicious analysis of arguably the most important and undervalued group of people in modern American society: married women as mothers. I say arguably because most of the modern "emancipated" women had lost their connection with the traditional role of wife and mother, not by accident, but by choice. The year 1936 could be 2011. Modern women were free—"free to serve machines, free to starve, free to go on the streets. There is little choice among such freedoms." They worked and provided for families, many because they had to, others because they chose to. Modern society dictated that course.

Fisher concluded that:

> Both men and women have better records as voters if they are married, if they own property, and if they have permanent residences. In other words, given the security which marriage and roots in one's own community afford, both men and women take their citizenship more seriously. When such security is possible for the majority of American citizens—when the people own America—then, and then only, will America become democratic. Women, too, will be citizens in that new democracy.

This was an indirect indictment of the modern woman, a woman who Fisher believed too "ignorant, bewildered, helpless or indifferent" to make a difference in the dizzying mess of modern society. The modern woman, Fisher argued, did not want to live in a genderless society, regardless of a gradual push in that direction. What she wanted most was to preserve humanity:

> These women do not want their husband's jobs; they do not want to take men's places. They want to be effective and responsible citizens, to contribute what they can to their communities. They do not want their children to grow up in big cities. They want for their children the kind of closeness to reality, the variety of experiences, the satisfaction of performing simple and necessary tasks, which they themselves knew in their childhood homes. They know that their children must be prepared to meet change, and they believe that there is no better preparation for it than to have roots, to have love for and faith in the homely things of life. They want them to have the courage to be themselves. They want them to create a free and democratic America.

In a time when women are told that liberty means fewer children and a career, Fisher's prescription for family and society seems quaint. But there is a growing trend in the United States of women moving back into traditional roles by having larger families and forgoing a career to be a mother and in many cases, through home-schooling, a teacher. Women have long been the standard bearer for the tradition and stability of society. They rear their children on the history and culture of their people, provide a link to the past, and nurture future generations to develop a respect for place and tradition. Fisher recognized that they were the key to cultural independence. Without winning that war, a "free and democratic America" cannot exist.

Hilaire Belloc's "The Modern Man" was a continuation on that theme, and as the concluding chapter to the book, it was an exclamation point on the destruction of the old order. Man, living in the modern industrialist state, had lost his connection with the past, his economic freedom, and his belief in the "old religious doctrines." This had created a "conception of himself which molds all of his actions." Man, in essence, had by inertia been dislocated from his traditional mores. He had no dock, no compass, and no map.

Before modern industrial society had robbed man of the good and the beautiful, men, as representative of society at large, "strongly" retained the "ancient doctrines" of their ancestors. This was grounded in religion, in the belief of free will, "the doctrine of immorality of the soul surviving death forever; the doctrine of the Incarnation . . . which gave to the personality of man an infinite values since it was so regarded by its Creator; and the doctrine of eternal reward and punishment." Man had instead substituted Christian values for "the worship of the community of which he is a member. There is a new religion which is not exactly the worship of the State, but the worship of the collective body . . . of which the individual is a member." As a result, man could reject religion, but he could not ridicule or reject the honor of the collective, what had become the state or empire. Man now worshiped man and his creation, not that of the Creator.

Belloc contended this shift allowed for the modern man to be reduced to a wage-slave, a tool at the hands of the plutocracy. Why? Because he had no conception of independence, and no attachment to the land. Modern society, the machine age, had made him weak, and the loss of tradition had made him intellectually unable to cope with or resist the drastic changes that usurped his independence:

> Now it should be clear to anyone who will think lucidly and coldly upon the direction in which all this must move that it is moving toward the re-establishment of slavery. . . . To be compelled to work, not by your own initiative, but at the initiative of another, is the definition of slavery. Whether slavery shall come first in the form of slavery to the State before it arrive at the final and natural and stable form of slavery to individuals—slavery it still is, and the modern man accepts such slavery in the unshakable belief that it is in the nature of things.

Belloc lamented that slavery was the least of man's worries, for the end result was the "decline of our civilization."

Belloc offered a Mass for the Resurrection. "The few who have perceived these truths, the few who can contrast the modern man with the immediate ancestry of his age, but have forgotten, know that the remedy can only be found in a change of philosophy; that is, of religion." Only by grounding man in the ancient order of things, including the possession of land, would man be able to restore his independence. The few who could see this were charged with carrying this task forward. Yet, "it was their duty to realize that this task has become exceedingly difficult of achievement, that the difficulty is increasing, and that therefore they must bear themselves as must all those who attempt a creative effort at reform: that is, as sufferers who will probably fail." In retrospect, Belloc composed what Russell Kirk labeled the "ten conservative principles" long before Kirk wrote them. Property, independence, a respect for the old order, an understanding that change and tradition had to be "reconciled," community and the imperfectability of the soul were part of Belloc's crusade to save man from himself. Cultural independence, Belloc suggested, breeds political and economic independence. We should listen and by listening become one of his suffering martyrs.

Those who considered *Who Owns America?* fascist or communist never read it, and those who classified it as un-American never understood American history. It is the practical application of the conservative mind, a prescription—political, economic, and cultural—for the restoration of the old American order. It is the culmination of centuries of wisdom, a philosophical critique, yes, but more a call to action, partly political, partly economic, and wholly cultural. Independence, the type of independence every sage in the preceding sixteen chapters advocated, can be achieved. It is the American way. It is distinctly American conservatism.

—Brion McClanahan

Bibliography

Agar, Herbert and Allen Tate, eds. *Who Owns America? A New Declaration of Independence.* Wilmington, Del.: Intercollegiate Studies Institute, 1999.

Borden, Morton, ed. *America's Eleven Greatest Presidents.* New York: Rand McNally, 1971.

Borden, Morton. *The Federalism of James A. Bayard.* New York: AMS Press, 1968.

Bradford, M. E. *Original Intentions: On the Making and Ratification of the Constitution*, Athens: University of Georgia Press, 1993.

———. *A Better Guide Than Reason: Federalists and Anti-Federalists.* New Jersey: Transaction Publishers, 1994.

———. *Founding Fathers: Brief Lives of the Framers of the United States Constitution.* Lawrence: University of Kansas Press, 1994.

Brooks, Cleanth. *On the Prejudices, Predilections, and Firm Beliefs of William Faulkner.* Baton Rouge: LSU Press, 1987.

———. *William Faulkner: Yoknatapawpha Country.* Baton Rouge: LSU Press, 1963.

Bruccoli, Matthew J., ed., *Just Representation: A James Gould Cozzens Reader.* Carbondale: Southern Illinois University Press, 1978.

Campbell, Karl E. *Senator Sam Ervin, Last of the Founding Fathers.* Chapel Hill: University of North Carolina Press, 2007.

Chappell, Absalom H. *Miscellanies of Georgia, Historical, Biographical, Descriptive, etc.* Columbus, Ga.: Thomas Gilbert, 1874.

Cheek, H. Lee, Jr., *Calhoun and Popular Rule.* Columbia: University of Missouri Press, 2004.

Chitwood, Oliver Perry. *John Tyler: Champion of the Old South.* New York: Russell and Russell, Inc., 1939.

Clancy, Paul R. *Just a Country Lawyer: A Biography of Senator Sam Ervin.* Bloomington: Indiana University Press, 1974.

Cole, Wayne S. *Charles A. Lindbergh and the Battle Against American Intervention in World War II.* New York: Harcourt Brace Jovanovich, 1974.

Cooper, James Fenimore. *The American Democrat*. New York: A. A. Knopf, 1931.

———. *The Littlepage Manuscripts: Satanstoe, The Chainbearer, and The Redskins*. New York: Stringer and Townsend, 1852.

Cozzens, James Gould. *Guard of Honor*.

———. *By Love Possessed*.

Ervin, Sam J., Jr. *Preserving the Constitution: The Autobiography of Senator Sam J. Ervin, Jr.*, Charlottesville, Va.: The Michie Company, 1984.

Foster, William O. *James Jackson, Duelist and Militant Statesman, 1757-1806*. Athens: University of Georgia Press, 1960.

Godkin, Edwin Lawrence. *Life and Letters of Edwin Lawrence Godkin*. 2 vols. New York: MacMillan, 1907.

———. *Reflections and Comments 1865-1895*. New York: Charles Scribner's Sons, 1895.

———. *Problems of Modern Democracy: Political and Economic Essays*. New York: Charles Scribner's Sons, 1896.

Kirk, Russell. *The Conservative Mind: From Burke to Eliot*. Chicago: Regnery, 1986.

Larson, Bruce L. *Lindbergh of Minnesota: A Political Biography*. New York: Harcourt Brace Jovanovich, 1971.

McClanahan, Brion. "A Lonely Opposition: James A. Bayard and the American Civil War." PhD diss., University of South Carolina, 2006.

Mencken, H.L. *Prejudices: A Selection*. New York: Vintage Books, 1958.

———. *The Vintage Mencken*. New York: Vintage Books, 1955.

Meriwether, James B., ed. *William Faulkner: Essays, Speeches, and Public Letters*. New York: Modern Library, 2004

Mosley, Leonard. *Lindbergh: A Biography*. New York: Doubleday, 1976.

Richardson, James D. *A Compilation of the Messages and Papers of the Presidents 1789-1897*. 10 vols. Washington, D.C.: Bureau of National Literature and Art, 1901.

Sumner, William Graham. *War and Other Essays*. New Haven: Yale University Press, 1911.

———. *The Forgotten Man and Other Essays*. New Haven: Yale University Press, 1907.

Tansill, Charles C. *The Congressional Career of Thomas F. Bayard*. New York: Fordham University Press, 1946.

Taylor, John. *An Inquiry into the Practices and Policy of the Government of the United States*. Fredericksburg, Va.: Green and Cady, 1814.

Taylor, John. *Construction Construed, or Constitutions Vindicated.* Richmond: Shepherd and Pollard, 1820.
Trask, H. Arthur Scott. "The Constitutional Republicans of Philadelphia, 1818-1848: Hard Money, Free Trade, and State Rights." PhD diss., University of South Carolina, 1998.
Twelve Southerners. *I'll Take My Stand: The South and the Agrarian Tradition.* Baton Rouge: Louisiana State University Press, 2006.
Upshur, Abel P. *A Brief Inquiry into the True Nature and Character of Our Federal Government.* Petersburg: Edmund and Julian C. Ruffin, 1840.
Welch, Richard E. *The Presidencies of Grover Cleveland.* Lawrence: University Press of Kansas, 1988.
Wilson, Clyde N., ed. *A Defender of Southern Conservatism: M.E. Bradford and His Achievements.* Columbia, Mo.: University of Missouri Press, 1999.
Wilson, Clyde N., ed., *The Essential Calhoun: Selections from Writings, Speeches, and Letters.* New Brunswick, N.J.: Transaction, 1991.

Index

Abolitionists, 26, 58
Adams, John Quincy, 37, 73
Adams, John, 25, 28, 30-32, 38-39, 45, 58
Adams, Samuel, 181-82
African Americans, 125-26, 153-54, 158, 161, 163-66, 181
America First Committee, 137-39
American Democrat, The, 49, 58
American "exceptionalism," 111, 117
"American System," 19, 63-65, 68-69, 71
Anti-Masonic party, 58
Anti-rent movement, 52-53
Arnold, Benedict, 87
Arthur, Chester A., 143

Baltimore, Md., 142-43
Banks and money, 28-29, 31, 61-71, 75, 88-90, 98-99, 103, 107, 112-15, 118, 122-23, 125, 129-36, 181. *See also* National Bank
Bayard family, 35-48
Bayard, James A. (elder), 35-36, 38-41, 44-45
Bayard, James A. (younger), 35, 37, 39-43, 45-48
Bayard, Thomas F. (Sr.), 35, 37, 39-40, 43-44, 46-47

Beard, Charles A., 27
Beecher, Henry Ward, 101-2
Belloc, Hilaire, 186-87
Bennett, William ("Blackjack"), 170
Biddle, Nicholas, 68
Blaine, James G., 121
Bork, Robert, 34
Boston, Mass., 19-20
Bradford, M. E., 139-40, 152, 169-78
British inheritance, 26, 28, 173, 175-77, 181-82
Brook Farm, 119
Brooks, Cleanth, 151, 153
Brown, John, 58, 120
Bryan, William Jennings, 61, 121, 143
Bryce, James, 121
Buchanan, James, 57, 97
Buckley, William F., 168
Buffalo, N.Y., 95-97
Burke, Edmund, 77, 153, 172, 175, 183
"Burnt-Over District," 58
Burr, Aaron, 38
Bush family, 143
By Love Possessed, 149-50

Calhoun, John C., 33-34, 85-94, 100, 126, 155

Capitalists as counter conservative, 13, 18-21, 26, 29-31, 34, 65, 71, 75, 106, 111-15, 123, 127, 129, 132, 136, 180-81, 186
Carey, Henry, 63
Carey, Matthew, 63, 70-71
Chinese exclusion, 102-3
Christianity, 37, 58, 101-3, 107, 148-49, 152-54, 159-60, 175, 181, 186-87
Civil rights legislation, 158-59, 163-66, 168
Civil War, U.S., 37, 39-43, 45-47, 64, 70-71, 95, 100-101, 107, 120-21, 130, 133, 142-43, 152-53, 158-59, 164, 171-73, 181-83
Clay, Henry, 56, 68, 73, 77-78, 85, 90
Cleveland, Grover, 37, 43, 95-103, 121
Coit, Margaret, 86
Connecticut, 54-57, 148, 175
Constitution for the United States, Abel P. Upshur on, 78-83; James and Thomas Bayard on, 44-48; John Taylor on, 27-34; M. E. Bradford on, 169-178; "necessary and proper" clause, 20, 29, 31, 65; "original intent" doctrine, 34; Sam Ervin on, 157-68; "sanctity of contracts" clause, 22; "strict construction" doctrine, 33-34, 182. *(The text is dense with discussions of the ratification and interpretation of the Constitution, the American Founding, and federalism too numerous to reference.)*

Coolidge, Calvin, 143
Cooper, James Fenimore, 49-59
Cooperstown, N.Y., 51-52
Corporations, 29, 33, 64-67, 127
Cozzens, James Gould, 147-50
Cromwell, Oliver, 48, 120

Davidson, Donald, 170, 179, 183-84
Davie, William R., 175
Davis, Jefferson, 57
Debs, Eugene V., 142
Debt, public, 11, 13, 18-21, 26, 28-29, 31, 62, 75, 88-89, 99, 111, 135-36, 162-63
Declaration of Independence, 17, 25, 27, 32, 42, 80, 154, 170, 172-73, 177
Delaware, *See* Bayard family.
Democratic party, 13, 40, 56-57, 69, 89-90, 95-97, 103, 121, 136, 143, 145, 157-68
Depressions, E.L. Godkin on, 122; Great, 134, 180; of 1819, 63, 66, 68
Dickinson, John, 174-75, 181
Disquisition on Government, 86
Douglas, Stephen A., 118
Dual sovereignty, 81
Duane, William J., 68-69
Dutch in New York, 36, 51-52
Duty, 17, 85, 87, 147-53, 164

Eisenhower, Dwight D., 164-66
Environmentalism, 179
Episcopal Church, 107, 148-49
Equality, 34-35, 39-40, 47-48, 51-52, 54, 65, 139-40, 172-73, 177
Ervin, Samuel J., 157-68

Evolution, 161

Faulkner, William, 142, 151-55, 170
Federal Reserve, 66, 133-35
Federalist, The, 32-33
Fisher, Mary Shattuck, 184-86
Fletcher v. Peck, 22
Foreign aid, 163
"Forgotten Man," 105-6, 108, 115, 127, 134
France, 40-41, 102, 175
Free trade. *See* Tariff
French Revolution, 30-31, 42-44, 62, 170, 172, 175

Garrett, George, 153
Genovese, Eugene D., 169
Georgia, 17-22
Gerry, Elbridge, 44
Godkin, Edward Lawrence, 117-27
Gouge, William, 64-65
Grant, U. S., 183
Guard of Honor, 149-50

Hamilton, Alexander, and Hamiltonianism, 19-21, 25-31, 37-39, 44-46, 61-62, 65, 74, 76, 89-90, 97-98, 107, 123, 130, 133, 163, 175, 177, 180, 183-84
Harding, Warren G., 134, 143
Harrison, William Henry, 56, 74, 77
Hawaii annexation, 101
Henry, Patrick, 115, 175, 181
Hobbes, Thomas, 162, 181
Hofstadter, Richard, 106-7
Hoover, Herbert, 143, 183

Huguenots, 36, 62
Hull, William, 87

I'll Take My Stand, 179-80
Ickes, Harold, 138-39
Immigration, 13, 22, 102-3, 118, 129-30
Imperialism, 12-13, 43-44, 48, 63, 70-71, 86-94, 101, 107-12, 118, 123-25, 134, 143-44, 183, 186
Ingersoll, Charles J., 64
"Internal improvements," 33, 56-57, 63, 66, 71, 74-76, 78-79
Irving, Washington, 51

Jackson, Andrew, 56-57, 66, 68-69, 73, 76, 83, 89-90, 107
Jackson, James, 17-23
Jackson, Thomas J., 120, 158
"Jacksonian democracy," 55-56, 69, 73-74
Jefferson, Thomas, 17, 20, 25-27, 30, 33, 38-39, 45, 57, 61, 74, 96-97, 101, 103, 135, 143, 172, 181-82
Jeffersonianism, 11, 25-34, 63, 65, 71, 73-75, 77-81, 83, 90, 95, 103, 107-8, 114-15, 130, 133, 135-36, 154-55, 159, 162-63, 168, 179, 181-83
Johnson, Lyndon B., 95

Kennedy family, 143, 158
Kentucky Resolutions, 25, 33
Kirk, Russell, 12-14, 26, 39, 77, 169, 171, 173-74, 176, 187

Lee, Robert E., 155, 158, 164
Lewis, C. S., 12

Liberals, according to H. L. Mencken, 143, 146; according to James Gould, Cozzens, 147; and Sam Ervin, 158, 168; and William Faulkner, 151-53
Lincoln, Abraham, 42, 57, 71, 77, 83, 86, 123, 126, 143, 169, 173, 181
Lindbergh, Charles A., Jr., 129-32, 137-40
Lindbergh, Charles A., Sr., 129-37
Littlepage Manuscripts, 51, 53-54
Locke, John, 181
Lodge, Henry Cabot, 143
Lytle, Andrew, 170

Maclay, William, 20
Macon, Nathaniel, 23
Madison, James, 20, 33, 37, 40-41, 81, 174-76, 184
Magna Charta, 160, 181
Majority rule, 30-31, 35, 39-40, 44-48, 50, 52-53, 55-56, 70-71, 82, 105-6, 108, 117-18, 125-27, 142-44, 177
Manifest Destiny, 43, 94
Markham, Edwin, 158
Marshall, John, 78
McClellan, James, 28
McDonald, Forrest, 17-18, 169
McKinley, William, 124
Mencken, Henry Louis, 49, 141-46
Meriwether, James B., 151
Mexican War, 86, 90, 93-94
Michigan, 87
Mill, John Stuart, 122
Milton, John, 181

Minnesota, 129-40
Mississippi, 21, 46, 151-55
Missouri Compromise, 86
Monroe Doctrine, 43-44, 101, 135
Monroe, James, 23, 62
"Moral imagination," 13
Mormons, 58
Morris, Gouverner, 175
Morris, Robert, 107

Napoleon I, 48
Nation, The, 121
National Bank, 20, 28-29, 56, 61, 63, 65-66, 68-69, 71, 74-78, 89
National Democratic Party ("Gold Democrats"), 121-23
National Endowment for the Humanities, 169-70
Native Americans, 51, 102-3
Neoconservatives, 11-12, 111, 140, 169-71, 173
New Deal, 142-46, 180, 183
New England, 18, 20, 39, 48, 51-52, 55, 64, 69, 119, 148. *See also* Yankee culture
New York City, N.Y., 20, 54, 119, 136, 147, 149, 183
New York, 49-59, 68-69, 96-97, 148
Newspapers, bad influence of, 47, 52, 56, 131-32, 134-35, 139
Nixon, Richard M., 158-59, 163, 166-67
North Carolina, 23, 157-68, 175
"Nullification," 25-26, 33-34, 70, 73, 75-77, 81-82, 91-92

Oregon Territory, 86, 93

Owsley, Frank L., 180-82, 184

Parker, Alton B., 103
Philadelphia, Pa., 21-22, 61-71
Philippines, 124-25
Pierce, Franklin, 57
Pitt, William, 77
Political parties, bad influence of, 13, 40, 48, 50, 52-58, 62, 88, 90-92, 96, 99, 103, 108, 113-14, 117-19, 121, 125, 141-43, 162-63
Polk, James K., 90, 93-94
"Prescription," 12, 176
President, U.S., and "executive privilege," 158-59, 166-67; and forms of address, 18-19; and veto, 68, 99, 167; and war powers, 93-94. *See also* Cleveland, Grover; Jackson, Andrew; Roosevelt, Franklin D.; Tyler, John.
Presidential elections, of 1800, 38-39; of 1840, 66, 77, 90; of 1844, 90; of 1860, 57; of 1884, 121-23; of 1896, 121-23
Progress, 34-35, 57-58, 93, 105-6, 115
Progressive party, 146
Progressivism, 97, 113, 130. *See also* reform and reformers
Public opinion, 50, 117, 119, 126, 129, 134-35
Public schools, 48, 54-55, 161
Puritans, 18, 54-55, 58, 120, 144

Raguet, Condy, 29, 61-71
Randolph, John, 22, 27
Reagan, Ronald, 11-12, 169-70

"Reconstruction," 37, 39-40, 45-47, 100-101, 122, 125-26, 152-53, 180
Reform and reformers, 55, 57-59, 96-97, 105-6, 113, 117, 130, 136, 141, 143, 146-47, 149, 173
Rent-seeking, 34, 62
Republican party, 12-13, 42, 45-47, 56, 70-71, 96, 101, 109, 120-21, 129-30, 136, 143, 161, 167, 181, 183
Republican virtue, 17, 19, 22, 27, 39-40, 87, 90, 92-93, 97
Ricardo, David, 64, 67
Ripley, George, 119, 121
Rockefeller family, 143
Roman, ancient, influence of, 17-18, 44-46, 85, 87-88, 124, 171-73
Roosevelt, Franklin D., 95, 98, 137-39, 144-46, 180
Roosevelt, Theodore, 44, 95, 130, 143-44
Rutledge, John, 175

Santo Domingo, 62
Savannah, Georgia, 18-19, 22
Say, Jean-Baptiste, 64
Schurz, Carl, 101
Scottish Enlightenment, 175
Secession, 41-42, 81
Seward, William H., 126
Sherman, Roger, 175
Silver coinage issue, 61, 99, 114, 122-23, 127
Sixties, the, 11, 150, 153
Slavery, 26, 33, 58, 62, 71, 73, 76, 85-86, 120, 152, 158, 187

Smith, Adam, 64
Smithson bequest, 87-88
Social Darwinism, 106-7
Socialism, 11, 58, 64, 105-6, 108, 113, 119, 127, 129, 132, 136, 142, 146, 180, 184, 187
Solzhenitsyn, Aleksandr, 50, 55
South Carolina, 13, 18, 23, 33, 70, 75-77, 153, 175
South, the, according to E. L. Godkin, 118-21; according to H. L. Mencken, 142-43; and Sam Ervin, 157-59, 163-64, 168
Southern Agrarians. *See* Bradford, M. E.; Taylor, John; *Who Owns America?*
Spanish-American War, 108-12, 123-25
Statue of Liberty, 102
Story, Joseph, 78-82
Sumner, William Graham, 105-15, 132
Sumter, Thomas, 18
Supreme Court, U.S., 13, 21-22, 30, 32, 34, 78-82, 122-23, 157, 162, 165, 182

Tariff, 19-21, 31, 56, 58, 62-64, 69-71, 74-78, 88-91, 98, 110, 113-15, 122-23, 125, 130, 180
Tate, Allen, 170
Taylor, John, 11, 23, 25-34, 49, 65, 98, 114, 132, 155
Texas, 46, 90, 93-94, 170
Tocqueville, Alexis de, 50, 58
Trask, H. A. Scott, 70
Treason, 32

Tyler, John, 56, 73-83, 86, 93

Upshur, Abel P., 73-83

Van Buren, Martin, 56, 68, 90
Vermont, 86
Vietnam War, 166
Virginia, 23, 25-34, 46, 73-83, 143

Wallace, Henry A., 146
War and conservatism, 12, 40-44, 92-94, 124, 129, 134-35, 138. *See also* Imperialism
War of 1812, 37, 40-43, 69, 86-87, 92
War of Independence, American, 17-23, 26-28, 49-51, 73, 77, 79-80, 115, 154, 159, 165, 167, 171-72, 174-75, 181-82
Washington, George, 17, 57, 78, 85, 97, 99, 101, 103, 167
Watergate, 157-59, 163, 167
Webster, Daniel, 73, 77-78, 85
Webster, Noah, 57
Whig party, 25, 52, 55-57, 69, 73-83, 89-90, 94
Who Owns America?, 179-88
Wilson, James, 21, 175
Wilson, Woodrow, 95, 97, 135, 143-44
Wirt, William, 78
Woman's suffrage, 125-26
Women in modern society, 184-86
Wood, Robert E., 137
World War I, 129, 134-36, 142, 144, 160

World War II, 129, 131-32, 137-40, 148-49, 153

Yankee culture, 48, 53-55, 58, 179, 183
Yazoo claims, 21-22